I HATE SCHOOL

I HATE SCHOOL

HOW A COLLEGE FOOTBALL COACH
HAS INSPIRED STUDENTS TO VALUE
EDUCATION AND BECOME
LIFELONG LEARNERS

COACH JOHN BAXTER

WITH CLINT STITSER

Advantage®

Published by Advantage, Charleston, South Carolina.
Member of Advantage Media Group.

ADVANTAGE is a registered trademark and the Advantage colophon is a trademark of Advantage Media Group, Inc.

Printed in the United States of America.

ISBN: 978-159932-429-6
LCCN: 2013946566

This publication is designed to provide accurate and authoritative information in regard to the subject matter covered. It is sold with the understanding that the publisher is not engaged in rendering legal, accounting, or other professional services. If legal advice or other expert assistance is required, the services of a competent professional person should be sought.

 Advantage Media Group is proud to be a part of the Tree Neutral® program. Tree Neutral offsets the number of trees consumed in the production and printing of this book by taking proactive steps such as planting trees in direct proportion to the number of trees used to print books. To learn more about Tree Neutral, please visit www.treeneutral.com. To learn more about Advantage's commitment to being a responsible steward of the environment, please visit www.advantagefamily.com/green

Advantage Media Group is a publisher of business, self-improvement, and professional development books and online learning. We help entrepreneurs, business leaders, and professionals share their Stories, Passion, and Knowledge to help others Learn & Grow. Do you have a manuscript or book idea that you would like us to consider for publishing? Please visit advantagefamily.com or call 1.866.775.1696.

To my wife Jill, who I must credit not only for naming the program "Academic Gameplan" in 1992 but for keeping it alive as a viable business venture since its copyright in 1999. A great mother, wife, partner, friend, attorney and business woman you have incredibly balanced our family, our finances and our business ventures masterfully. It is with great pride that I recognize that our work with "The Academic Gameplan" would have gained no traction and had no impact without your dedication to the concept. To you goes my most heartfelt and deepest Thank You.

To all of the coaches that have defined and shaped my life both as mentors and co-workers. I truly believe that a coach is a person who takes someone where they are unable to take themselves. I was taught that the term "COACH" is a term of endearment. It's a title that you can never take lightly and one that you have to earn every day.

—JOHN BAXTER

FOREWORD

John Baxter is a teacher. The fact that he is one of the country's best and most innovative football coaches is incidental to the fact that he is a teacher first, last, and in between.

As the athletic director at the University of Southern California, I have had the pleasure of working with John the past three years. He is the most remarkable special teams football coach I have met in over 40 years involved in the game of football. What makes John so different, so special, is his ability to teach and relate to young men and help them with their academic and life success.

Wherever John has coached, his Academic Gameplan has helped launch hundreds of young football players' successful academic careers. I have seen it here at USC. I have seen John's passion firsthand, sometimes attending his Academic Gameplan meetings (which often start at 6:30 a.m.!) at which his students, who happen to be some pretty darn good football players, learn some of life's lessons particularly well. His plan also prepares them for the rigors of a first-rate college education.

His success has been phenomenal, both at Fresno State and now at USC. John is one very special person and teacher. We are lucky to have him at USC and I believe that anyone who reads his book will understand why Coach Baxter and his students have been so successful in life and in athletics.

—PAT HADEN

Pat Haden, a Rhodes Scholar, was a two-time National Championship Quarterback at the University of Southern California and quarterback of the NFL Los Angeles Rams before becoming a lawyer, a successful businessman, and football broadcaster. He assumed the athletic directorship at his alma mater on Aug. 3, 2010. He quarterbacked the 1972 and 1974 national championship USC Trojans, and was quarterback for the Los Angeles Rams from 1976 to 1981. He holds a BA degree, magna cum laude, from USC, where he was a Phi Beta Kappa; a BA degree in economics from Oxford University as a Rhodes Scholar; and a juris doctorate from Loyola Law School. He is a partner at Riordan, Lewis & Haden, a private equity law firm based in Los Angeles.

TABLE OF CONTENTS

Why I

"HATE"

School

Complete this phrase: I ____ school!

Why is this phrase almost always completed the same way? The overwhelming number-one response is "hate." When I ask adults over the age of 25, or young people under the age of nine, they often say they like it, love it, or enjoy it. When I ask almost any person of middle-school through college age, he or she invariably responds with the same word: *hate!* In fact, if you try this yourself you will find that people are moderate when they give their response because their gut feeling tells them to fill in the word *hate*, but they have a difficult time owning those feelings.

As adults reflect on school, they recall many good memories and experiences. By comparison to adult life, it was a time of carefree exuberance, friends, and fun. By contrast, young people ages 12 to 21 are still dealing with the day-to-day stress and pressure of school. It seems like a never-ending, low-grade headache.

It's only in retrospect that we begin to appreciate the experience and see the value of our school years. Most adults come to see that school was just a warm-up to the stresses to come, as a parent, a professional, a coworker, a provider, a community servant—as any of the many roles of adult life.

From the student's perspective, education and everything about it feels like a stream of orders and demands. People don't buy into orders, but they do buy into ideas. They buy into a purpose. It is very rare that someone helps students become connected to the purpose, value, and idea behind their education. Rather, they are told they must study "because I said so," or because "this is just the way it is" or some version of those.

Technology is a tool. Correctly using a tool requires technique. Yet we are doing the worst job in human history of teaching our children the technique and discretion necessary to be successful with the technology available. In the political climate of "no child left behind," education has become an environment of testaholics and curriculum snobs. Teachers are forced to "teach to the test," while students obligingly respond, amid constant technology interruptions and mindless addiction to an unending stream of "content," valuable or not. All the while, our schools are sticking to the patterned activities that do not lead to a basic understanding of face-to-face human interaction, creative problem solving, and overall competitiveness.

All of us, young or old, will tend to hate anything that we believe has no true and valuable purpose. Many students have come to hate school because:

- they feel that they are simply following orders;
- they haven't discerned a purpose for their education;
- they aren't learning why or how to be students.

It is more important than ever that we connect young people to the purpose and outcome of any and all instruction—and that we teach the technique and discretion required to correctly use technology and be an effective student.

We must develop students who are thinkers, communicators, and competitors. That is what education is about. They need a coach, and a coach's role is to mentor, to direct, and to take students where they are unable to take themselves. If they could take themselves there, they wouldn't need a coach. Coaches coach. Players play. They need a plan for their lives, and it's my job to help co-create and execute this plan.

This book is for students, for anyone who has been a student, for any parent who has a student, and for anybody who knows a student and is invested in his or her success. The help that I offer is not just for college athletes. *It's for all students,* past, present, and future, who care about doing well in school and ultimately, in life.

The only role that football has played in the development of Academic Gameplan (AGP) is that the students I see every day just happen to be football players.

I presented my first Academic Gameplan seminar in 1999. It was for a group of students who weren't football players. In marketing the seminar, I did a talk-show promotion on a radio station that had carried our football games, and callers soon were jamming the phone lines to the football office. I didn't realize how much the message would resonate. So many people identified with the need.

The first question I heard from the callers was, "Who is this program for?" One caller wanted to bring an eight-year-old to the seminar, and another hoped to bring a fifth-grader. Yet another said: "I don't have any kids. I just want to come and listen." The program was designed for teens and young adults, and I couldn't promise that

I could keep a little kid engaged for the length of a seminar, but the message to me was clear: This program could serve everybody, regardless of age. So I gave it a try.

The feedback after the seminar was highly encouraging. "That was one of the best days I've ever spent with my kid," one person said. "We're talking like we've never talked before." Another said he owned a business and had begun incorporating the principles from the seminar in training employees as part of a strategic plan.

It wasn't just parents who brought their kids to the seminar. People brought their grandchildren, and their neighbors' kids. Youth coaches brought their team. From about age 12 on up, the message resonated across the board. They all seemed to see themselves in what I was talking about.

In short, Academic Gameplan is for students, and their parents, and anyone else who wants success in his or her own life or for someone he or she cares about. It's for those who have decided they won't be "waiting for Superman."

I highly recommend the 2010 documentary by that name, directed by Davis Guggenheim and produced by Lesley Chilcott. *Waiting for Superman* is about the horrendous condition of education. As public schools fail their children, people wait and hope they will win a lottery for a scarce opportunity to get them into a charter school where the fundamentals are taught. How long will we wait for some mythical superhero to swoop in to save the students? These problems will perpetuate until we do something different. The film outlines the problem clearly and dramatically. Nobody outlines a solution.

In Academic Gameplan, we're offering people a solution—and it's one that they just don't get in school.

I too hate school. That is, I hate how schools are overpromising and under delivering. I truly believe we are missing the mark in education. I consistently see students come in unprepared and leave unprepared to be competitive in life. It is my desire that this book generates questions about education that you should demand answers to.

If not you, then who?

To borrow a line from the movie *Network:* "I'm mad as hell, and I'm not going to take it anymore!"

And neither should you!

—COACH JOHN BAXTER

CHAPTER 1

Who COACHES the Student?

"Let's get one thing straight," I said, looking into the eyes of the young athlete I had come to see. "This is college football. It's not football college."

I was sitting with him and his father at the dining room table of their home in Reno, Nevada. I'd come from Fresno for this visit, and I told him what I'd told so many other high-school student athletes I've recruited in my three decades as a college football coach.

This particular young man, to whom I will introduce you soon, may not have needed to hear that quite as much as many of those I've recruited. But it's a point I always emphasize when I make home visits and get the opportunity to sit down with the family. I often see stars in their eyes, not just in the recruit, but in

BAXTERISM

This is college football. It's not football college.

the proud parents. They expect that I've come to talk about football, and the glories of the gridiron, and how great their kid will be for our school.

It feels like a culmination of their work and dreams. The boy's getting recruited, and here comes a scholarship. But in truth it's just the beginning. This is the entrance to college, to young adulthood, to a world of responsibilities and challenges.

In some homes, I'll sit with the young man and his mom, or dad, or both. Sometimes brothers and sisters come out and listen, or they whisper in a side room. The family is getting a visit, after all, by a coach from a program that has had 160 All-Americans, eleven national championships, seven Heisman trophy winners, and more players drafted than any school in the history of college football. It seems like such a momentous occasion.

We start to talk about opportunities, choices, and points of difference. We will have offered a scholarship, but the young man and his family are also entertaining the possibility of other scholarships. I begin to lay out our program and how our university would serve him and the role he would play in our football program. And then I pull out the young person's transcript and make it clear that college comes with football—he's there to study and to learn—and not just more about the game.

"Real champions love the work. Wannabes love the idea," I say to my players regularly. "Hey guys, it's not about the hype; it's about the prep." And that's what these home visits really are all about. The players and the parents may have visions of athletic greatness, but what I do is make it clear what it will take to achieve success. A lot of coaches, in home visits, play up the glory and the bright lights. I have a different perspective. I know what works in the long run. I am there to help young people envision the kind of future they really want but might not know how to reach.

Talking about football is not the main reason for my visits to these young people. I'm there to start building relationships, because without that, little else matters. That's what it truly means to be a coach: to help young people build a game plan for their lives.

SOMETHING "TO FALL BACK ON"?

Young athletes are chasing a dream. But that dream must be rounded, which is something that well-meaning adults tell them all the time.

At speaking engagements for my Academic Gameplan program, I ask people to complete this sentence: "Make sure that you stay in school and work hard and get your degree, because just in case football or athletics doesn't work out, someday you'll have something to _____." Invariably, people complete the sentence this way: "fall back on."

That's what they've heard; that's what they've been taught to believe. That's the paradigm you hear repeated over and over. And it's false. If you're falling back, you're going in the wrong direction. Think about it: in athletics, or in life, is there ever a time that you would want to fall back? No. Nor is a there time in any career when falling back is the preferred route. We should desire our education to propel us forward at all times. And if you want to take the proactive approach to empowering your child to succeed, please go to www.agp101.com.*

Every year, Coach Pat Hill, one of my closest friends and colleagues, told our seniors that "today's cheers are tomorrow's echoes." In other words, he's saying that the cheers and fame are hollow, and

---

* *See page 175 for a special offer.*

you need to leave with something of substance: An education that truly will last a lifetime.

In recruiting visits, when I sit down with families, we begin with the end in mind. I talk about where we want to go, and the role that the young man will need to play both athletically and academically. I explain that he will need strength and conditioning in both. He will need to learn technique and fundamentals. I am there to talk about the future of a young man and the prospects of his success, and not necessarily on a football field. I'm talking about long-term successes, not glories that are going to last for a few years. "You are going to be a student athlete," I say, "and as such you will be an athlete for a small part of your life, but you are going to be a student for the rest of your life."

I certainly don't want to crush a young man's vision of football fame. We once held a camp for inner city youth in New Orleans. We had prominent guest speakers: judges, doctors, lawyers, NFL players. They all told the kids to stay in school and do a good job in the classroom because football's not going to last forever. Then they quoted the harsh statistics on how many people play the game and how few make it to the professional level. Yes, the odds are against them, but the reason there are odds is because somebody can beat them. If someone cannot beat the odds, there would be no odds. Young athletes come to a camp like that to have fun and develop a dream. A dream is important, and no one has the right to take that away from anyone.

My goal is to replace that "falling back" paradigm with one that is more powerful and more motivating. You want to pursue an education and degree because you need balance in your life. Imagine yourself in a rowboat with one oar. You end up going in circles. But if you have two oars, you can head straight to your destination, steering left or right as you need. You have full control of that boat. Competing in the classroom as well as in athletics are the two oars I'm talking about.

Good coaching nurtures balance, when I visit the home of a young athlete and we sit at the table, I'm there to talk about the person, not the game. I'm there to talk about life skills and having a definite plan in place to develop the young person in all areas with a sense of purpose, heading for success and not struggle. In our finances, we are told to balance and diversify our portfolios to protect against risk and market volatility. I help young people balance their portfolio of life experiences. I want to make sure they have more than one oar in the water so that they can steer.

I mentor young people as if they were my own children. I'm always talking about a much bigger picture than they have in mind because they don't have enough experience to see it. I talk to them from the start about the importance of sound decision-making. I tell them it is like driving a car. Your hand must be on the steering wheel to keep it on course but 99 percent of the time you are off course. You must constantly make adjustments to stay on course. The car cannot drive itself. Life is like that. You come to a curve in the road, or to a fork, and your adjustments and decisions lead you to your destination. In fact, knowing that destination is how you choose your path.

WHAT IS ACADEMIC GAMEPLAN?

"Student athlete" is the politically correct term we use to describe our players. Examining the two words, we ask two fundamental questions. Who teaches an athlete how to play a game? When I ask that question at seminars, most people have a quick answer: a coach. But they grope for an answer when I ask the second question:

"Who teaches the student how to study?" Some venture to say it's the teacher. No, a teacher focuses on his or her specific subject, at least in the years after elementary school. Some say it's the parents. But when the child comes home and says he didn't do anything that day and has no homework, a parent is rendered helpless.

Essentially, what Academic Gameplan has grown into is this: It is the rules, fundamentals, and techniques to the game of school. I know intuitively as a coach that if you don't teach rules, fundamentals, and technique, you don't win. The best teachers of any game—football, basketball, golf—are always admired for their mastery of the fundamentals.

Young people will be making many important decisions, and among the first of them at this point will be where they want to go to college. They may have no idea what they are looking for: the type of programs, large campus or small, close to home or far away. Lacking any clarity about their destination, they often resort to making what amounts to an impulse buy. Instead, they should be looking at points of difference—that is, the factors that distinguish one campus from another and what matters most to them.

For athletes, a major factor will be who they want to coach them, and if they play for a coach like me, one thing is certain: they are going to go through Academic Gameplan, in keeping with my core message about their chief purpose for being in college.

At most colleges, the academic enrichment program amounts to "study hall." At the first sign that an athlete is slipping academically, it's off to study hall in the hope that he or she can bring up those grades so as not to be declared ineligible. The prescription is to study harder, and it's a prescription that's only given once the symptoms develop. The coaches see their job as teaching the sport, and if the students aren't making it the rest of the way, well, then they had better buckle down.

And so they're shipped off to study hall, perhaps with an assistant coach as the proctor, and they're told to get in there and study—in other words, to do what they don't know how to do. If they knew how, they wouldn't need to be there. Back in 1986, when I was a graduate assistant coach at Iowa State, I had that duty. I was a study hall monitor. It saddens me to think that with all the education and enlightenment and technology today, the only thing we can come up with for academic development is study hall.

When I'm recruiting athletes, I point out that we don't do study hall. Instead, we teach them how to play the game of school. In a large sense, Academic Gameplan is a game plan for life. Invariably, at some point in the program, one of the guys raises his hand and announces, as if he's had an epiphany: "You know what, Coach, this isn't just for school. This is something I can use anywhere, wherever I go!" To which I respond: "Oh, really! Tell me more…"

THIS IS COLLEGE FOOTBALL, NOT FOOTBALL COLLEGE

We point out to them that in our recruiting process of a Division 1 athlete, we are choosing from the top 1 percent of players, but that even with that quality of player, they would be annihilated in every game if we just tossed them the keys to the practice field and told them, "Okay, go out there and practice and we'll see you at game time." See, it's about technique, not talent. That holds true for athletics, and it holds true for academics. They have to know that, as young student athletes, everything they do relies on execution, academically and athletically. This is college football, not football college, and your success is going to be determined by how well you execute both roles.

We emphasize these things during the home visit because we're trying to get these young people to value our points of difference and see that we have a complete plan and an envisioned future for them that is much broader than what they have for themselves. That's why we emphasize the importance of decision making: Do they want to go to a school that emphasizes study hall, or do they want to come here, where we actually have a plan to develop them as individuals? The parents too are impressed by our approach, but we are not doing this to impress the parents; we're doing this because it's right. There's a poster in my office that reads, "Doing the right thing isn't always easy, but it's always right."

Often, in the recruiting process, an athlete will hear something like this: "You're a good player and you're going to be a big asset to our team, and sure, you need to go to school, but we'll make sure you get plenty of study hall and tutoring if it turns out you need that." Instead, we say this: "Sure, you're a good player, but you're not great (meaning you're not a finished product yet), and that's what we can make you. We'll bring out your strengths and drill you on the techniques, and people like you will help our program grow as you grow. But it's a team sport, and no one person is the team. And above all, you're in college to learn and develop as a person. Certainly, you have great potential, or we wouldn't be here having this talk. The key to success is learning to take care of your business, to efficiently handle your matters, and to execute in all areas of your life. If you fall behind academically, you not only risk ineligibility, but the stress level and self-doubt that comes from underperforming will certainly compromise your success on the field."

In Academic Gameplan we identify your strengths and drill you on the techniques and fundamentals. There is a famous proverb upon which we base Academic Gameplan, and that is, "If I give you a fish, you will eat today, but if I teach you to fish you will eat every day"—and that's our philosophy. We want young people to become fully independent and highly competitive in all areas of life.

A COACH'S TRUE ROLE REACHES FAR BEYOND SPORTS

Coaching isn't so much about sports as it is about mentoring. Frankly, I find sports to be boring to just watch. I prefer to be in the game. You have to get going in life, not just sit in front of the TV. My job as a coach is to develop young people to be their very best.

That's what parents should do too. A man and a woman can bring a child into the world, but true parenting is mentorship. It's guidance. Parents should create opportunities, encouraging and correcting along the way. And after thirty years of college coaching, I'm proud to see the fruits of my labor: young people who have become excellent husbands, parents, and successful business people.

The author Mitch Albom quotes Henry Adams in *Tuesdays with Morrie:* "A teacher affects eternity; he can never tell where his influence stops." I live every day by that. A coach deals individually with a young person even more than a teacher does. A college professor may see a student for an hour three days a week, perhaps, as part of a large class, but a coach sees that student virtually every day for five years.

The relationship between a coach and player often progresses the way that it does between a parent and child. It doesn't end, but it separates. You go on to other pursuits. It's a deep relationship and a significant role, and it enhances the role of the parent. Invariably, at some point during a home visit, I'll make a point, and Dad or Mom will tap the kid and say, "Now, don't I tell you that all the time!" And I'm sure they do. But when you hear something all the time, it becomes like white noise in the background. You tend to tune it out until a third party comes in and says the same thing.

> ## BAXTERISM
> The universal principal of coaching is, "the neighbor always has to tell your kid to choke up on the bat."

I'm that person. Often I'm just saying the same things the parents say, but the young person finally hears it. A father can teach his son to play baseball, but my experience has shown me that the universal principal of coaching is, "the neighbor always has to tell your kid to choke up on the bat." It's biblical. You cannot be a prophet in your own town!

After my home visits with an athlete, there should be nothing unclear about who I am as a coach and what I represent and what it will mean to be that young person's coach.

OUR SCHOOLS HAVE SADLY FAILED

In recruiting, we believe that you get what you bait your hook for. If we're looking for well-rounded people who really do want a good academic and athletic future, we believe we should lay all that out to them in their homes. People gravitate toward what excites them. If all someone wants from college is the fancy uniform and his name on a jersey, he doesn't

> ## BAXTERISM
> It's not about the hype, it's about the prep.

end up with us. He won't align with coaches like us, because, it's not about the hype, it's about the prep and the work. It has become a core belief of mine that true champions love the work and want-to-be's love the idea.

Most schools and most sports programs across the country have sadly failed our young people. They haven't emphasized what matters most: turning young people into thriving adults. Athletics has become the opiate of our society, and some people almost seem to live their lives through these athletes. They hover over the television, game to game to game. I spend no time watching sports on TV. If I have the time to watch sports, I have the time to play sports. I want the opportunity to compete.

BAXTERISM

Champions love the work and want-to-be's love the idea.

With the glorification of sports, athletics gets to the point where it comes first and everything else comes second. We often hear coaches talking about helping athletes become eligible, but unfortunately, when we strive for eligibility, we are striving for a minimum standard.

Instead, we need to go far beyond what it takes to be eligible. We need to bring out competitive greatness both on the sports field and in the classroom.

CHAPTER 2

Meeting

CLINT STITSER

The young man I'd come to visit in Reno on that cold, snowy day in 2003 was Clint Stitser, and today, a decade later, he is the director of student outreach and business development for Academic Gameplan.

I met with him and his father, Conrad, the year that Clint graduated from high school. I was recruiting for Fresno State, and Clint had survived to that point in the process. Hundreds of names of player prospects cross our desks, and we evaluate transcripts and film and begin to whittle the list down.

In every business relationship there is a buyer and a seller, and when I'm recruiting I always ask: "Which one are you?" Usually, the athlete says he's the buyer. "That's interesting," I say, because I'm here to offer you a scholarship, so wouldn't I be the buyer since I'm getting something for my money?" Recruiting involves a unique business relationship because there are two buyers and two sellers. The athlete is in the market to buy a college education and a sports opportunity. But the athlete also is doing a sales pitch with his transcript and film and how he presents himself as we talk. As the recruiter, I'm interested in "selling" him on the program, but I'm also "buying" talent with a scholarship.

Clint was a very strong student in high school with excellent grades. I know he was considering Missouri, Arizona State, and Stanford. If you had asked his dad where he should go, he would have said wherever he felt he'd have the best opportunities. If you had asked his mom, Cathy, she would have given one answer: Stanford. Done deal.

Often, when it gets down to making a decision, there is a champion in the young person's life who helps with the direction and the decision. The dad will have an agenda; the mom will have an agenda; the student will have an agenda; and the brothers and sisters will have an agenda. So will friends. Everybody starts telling the young person what would be best.

Clint had been getting mostly As, a few Bs, and he showed a strong character and work ethic. When I visited his high-school coach, I sat down for about six hours and watched every play of Clint's senior year. He always played with good effort. He played free safety in high school on a state championship team. He was a team captain and kicked off and kicked field goals. He also did other sports, and he snow boards, he wake baords, and he was a gymnast. Clint had an overall balanced, competitive portfolio.

Academically, it was obvious that he would succeed. Not every young person is going to graduate Phi Beta Kappa, and sometimes a coach needs to consider whether the prospect will be competitive academically or be an eligibility risk. Clint was no such risk. He was smart, strong, and balanced. Still, he was one of many young people I've helped to become thriving adults by coaching them in the fundamentals of life.

"YOU'RE A C+, MAYBE A B-"

As I sat at the dining room table that day with Clint and his father, who is a really good athlete and a phenomenal parent, I gave them my true assessment.

"You know, as a student, you're very competitive," I said. "Any university would want you. But as a football player, when I look at your numbers and kickoffs and field goals, well, you're a C-plus. Maybe a B-minus. Of the hundreds of players I've recruited, that's where you fall." Of course Clint was only "average" when compared with that select few, the cream of the high-school crop. It's not a word that a young athlete with dreams of glory wants to hear, but I think Clint took it as an inspiration and challenge. In fact, I found out years later that the comment really made him mad.

Clint had phenomenal success in college as an athlete, and as a starter he contributed to our tremendous team success. He graduated in four years with a degree in finance and a perfect 4.0, and he started his MBA before he even graduated. He had straight As. He never made one B in college. At graduation he was the dean's medalist, the valedictorian, in the Craig School of Business at Fresno State. Within a year he had his MBA, with another perfect 4.0, and was recognized as the exemplary student in that program.

I point all that out by way of answering all those people who often tell me, when they hear about Academic Gameplan, that it sounds like such a great program for the underachieving, at-risk student. That's not what we're all about. The program is for every student, because we are trying to take each to the highest level possible.

Clint exemplifies those students who reach for that level. He had his MBA in five years with perfect grades, and he played football at the highest possible level for his age, which was in Division 1. And then he got an opportunity to play in the National Football League and spent the next four or five years making that dream happen. Today he is married with two kids and has a great career in real estate. Clint made it.

WHEN THE OFFERS STOP COMING

Many young athletes haven't followed that path. In high school or in college, if they get cut from the team, basically, their football career is over. And if they make it as professional athletes, the question becomes: Who finances the dream? These guys get cut, but they hold on for another opportunity. And maybe they go a week, maybe a month, maybe two months, and somebody gives them another opportunity. And that's not unlike giving a drug addict another fix. They hemorrhage money while they wait for opportunity. Eventually, they just don't get any more calls, but the bills still need to be paid. And so they start as entry-level employees in whatever field they choose to go into.

It happens over and over to athletes. They start their careers and their life's work late. Most guys, once they're done with football, have to redefine themselves, and that's why so many go into broadcasting. They don't know who else they can be or what else they can be. They have competed at the highest level, under pressure, with millions watching, yet most come out and are lost. Some do build on those life skills and thrive, but many are left asking themselves, "What am I going to do now? What do I have to fall back on?" They may be into their 30s at that point and have to compete against people who have been in the work force for several years, with a lot more experience and networking time.

These athletes have much to contribute, but they don't necessarily recognize it. They have spent years waiting for the next opportunity to come to them. That's not the way it works in the rest of the world. In business and industry, you seek out opportunity. You find it. But in the NFL, you prepare and you wait. You train in anticipation of a day that may or may not be coming. Are you preparing for next week, next month, next season? You don't know for sure, but you have to be ready because the call could come tomorrow, at 9 a.m. or at midnight. Or it might never come. The money hemorrhage begins, and the money drains away, and you are in debt, and you find yourself in your 30s in an entry-level position.

Clint didn't let that happen. In his years as an athlete, he was also focused on progressing in his marketing and business development. His academic success afforded him the resources to support his athletic training; he financed his dream in a way that most athletes are unable to do. He was able to spend more time kicking, lifting, stretching, focusing, visualizing, traveling the country to tryouts, while still making enough money to support a young family. He did not put his life on hold as he waited for a dream. He was in the boat with both oars firmly in hand, pulling on them as hard as he could and rowing straight ahead.

A PORTRAIT OF OUR SUCCESS

What I saw in Clint was what Academic Gameplan aims to produce. He's the portrait of a thriving young adult. He has done well personally and professionally, as a family man, athlete, and in business. He had a good start and ran with it. He can tell you, though, about teammates who also have found success, yet didn't have such a good start academically. They had barely been eligible for college but thrived under our program. They gained skills for school and skills for life. Football is what brought them to us, but the academic advantage was their big payoff. That's so valuable in the long run that by comparison it makes the athletics seem like some kind of loss leader that lured them into college.

I am the product of five coaches: Frank Amato, Chuck Erlanbaugh, Fred Wright, Bob Bierie, and Ralph Micheli. They changed my life forever. They took me where I was unable to take myself. When I was discouraged, they showed me a future that I couldn't envision for myself. When I was encouraged, they supported me, and when I was wrong, they got me back in line. They were blessings put into my life. That's what I want for those I coach. I want to be a lasting influence in their lives.

In my years in athletics, I have coached thousands of young men. I'm not going to say I have my favorites, just as few parents would really admit to that, but some of those relationships have grown deeper over the years. When he was an undergraduate, Clint and I talked a lot about his future. Any coach would have appreciated his attitude and ethic. When I started talking, Clint started writing. When I laid out a program, he was all ears. But yet he wasn't a yes man either; he didn't hesitate to say, "I don't buy that," and to tell me what he thought. Our relationship grew, and I enjoyed watching his success.

THE PHONE CALL OF A LIFETIME

And then I got a telephone call from Clint in the spring of 2013, and that was 10 years, almost to the day, since we had met. That's significant to me because I often tell my players when I'm teaching them, "I am not talking to you right now; I am talking to you ten years from now," because someday it will all make sense to them. It was the greatest phone call of my life because it showed the ultimate in respect that a player can show a coach.

BAXTERISM

I am not talking to you right now; I am talking to you ten years from now.

In March 2013 the Detroit Lions called him with a great opportunity. The new staff at the Lions had long indicated that they would be interested in him if he were available and they had the position to fill. So all the stars seemed to be aligned for Clint on this one. It was a great opportunity to continue his football career. Thousands of young men dream of getting such a call. It's the moment that changes lives forever. It leads to being on the same field as the legends of the sport. For most players in Clint's position, the call would have been gold.

But he decided against it. Instead, he called me that day and told me he had decided he wanted to work with me on expanding Academic Gameplan. That's how much he believed in our work.

The program has been my way, as a college coach, of changing the paradigm. I do not overpromise and underdeliver. If anything, I do the opposite. I strive to serve the young people in my charge. It happens to be that the students I deal with are athletes, but young people all face the same challenges, no matter where they're from, urban or rural, anywhere in the land. My thirty years of coaching has taught me that. Teachers learn as much from their students as the students learn from them, it seems.

Clint has an in-depth knowledge of Academic Gameplan. After all, he has been through it himself, and he brings to it his finance and marketing background to help us reach out, to spread the word. He's the embodiment of the success of the program. And he represents, for me, the truth of those words that I tell so many kids on the first home visit: they'll come to appreciate what I'm saying in a decade, when they have experienced life and can handle it.

It was just a five-minute call, but it showed that Clint had learned clarity in his decision making. He took the reins in his own hands. He redirected his career and turned toward something that had played a significant role in his life. By the time he called me, he already knew what he wanted to do. He called to tell me about it. We had been talking about further developing Academic Gameplan, and his call was to say, "Let's get going."

At the end of this chapter and most of the other chapters in this book, you'll hear directly from Clint in his Field Note commentaries. I want you to hear not just my views but also the perspective of a man who has come through the program itself. He knows what it's like as a player and as a student. His family had high expectations of all their children. Other families lack that entirely. In a broad range of students, I have seen a clear failure to grasp the academic fundamentals. Together, Clint and I will explain why it is imperative that we change that.

— CLINT'S FIELD NOTE —

It was 3 a.m. I had just finished watching *Waiting for "Superman"* and I immediately fired off an e-mail to Coach Baxter blurting out what was on my mind. "I'm outraged!" I wrote, and I added a few paragraphs to make sure he knew just how much. When I finished watching, that's how I felt.

He had asked me to watch the documentary to get my feedback and reaction to the problems outlined in the film, and to see where I stood on the issues presented. In retrospect, it's obvious that the assignment was to ensure that my focus was in line with the values of Academic Gameplan. To me, the film is about families in need of hope as their kids go to "dropout factories." They look for that hope in charter schools that teach the fundamental skills that other schools don't. But the only way these people get their kids into these charter schools is by lottery. As outlined in the movie, there's a preponderance of proof that charter schools work, yet they are hardly proliferating and are still very limited. Imagine having to put your hope for your child's success in life on the outcome of a lottery.

I had decided at that point to pursue what mattered most, and passing up the chance to play with the Detroit Lions was one of the hardest decisions I've ever made. A kicker's options are limited. The teams don't have backups. They don't have two or three kickers. Each team carries one. In the Fortune 500, there are 500 chief executives. There are thirty-two jobs in the NFL for a placekicker, and thousands of college graduates dream about getting one of them. And there I was, on the short list for the Detroit Lions. How could I give up a dream I'd had for so long?

I've learned that football is really about developing yourself and learning the responsibilities of teamwork. I had a lot more to live for, and achieve in my life, than kicking a ball. My decision was to work with Academic Gameplan. It had more meaning to me than football, and I felt more passionate about it. I'd seen what it did for me and for those around me, and we must spread the message. I want to make an impact greater than I can make in football or in real estate. It's that simple.

Coach Baxter said this to me on the way to the airport, after we came to an agreement to work together: "Look, I'm the same guy and I'm going to stand for the same things whether I'm at USC, whether I'm at Fresno State, or whether I'm pushing a shopping cart and living under that bridge. " We were sitting in traffic on one of the L.A. freeways, and he pointed to an overpass. I believed him. He had done the same thing year in and year out with so many players, of all types. He says the same thing, with the same intensity, with the same meaning, and the same goal, which is to help young people achieve their full potential. He's a man of his word.

Locker rooms are full of chatter. The athletes compare notes. If what the coaches are saying is inconsistent with what they said a year ago, a month ago, or even last week, they lose credibility. The athletes stop listening. They stop buying in, and soon they stop playing 100 percent. Once that happens, you stop winning football games. There's a lesson for parents there: say what you mean; mean what you say.

Coach Baxter says it well. He has a way of boiling down complex ideas into quotes and sayings that stick with you for a lifetime. As players, we jokingly called them "Baxterisms," These are statements that have developed significant meaning in our lives but they flow out of him as undisputed truths. Truth be told, Coach didn't even realize he had "Baxterisms" until just a couple years ago because it was a concept we created as players. Oddly enough, when I talk to guys who played before and after me, we all end up referencing the same lines and points. These coaching points are extremely valuable nuggets, so much so, that I asked Coach to mark them throughout the book, because leaving you to find them on your own would be [BAXTERISM] "a violation of the anti-simplicity rule". When I was a student, some of what he told us didn't sink in (remember, he told us he was talking to us ten years from now). Today I keep having these epiphanies in which his words come back to me. The process has worked; I'm where he said I would be ten years ago.

BAXTERISM

That's a violation of the anti-simplicity rule.

CHAPTER 3

Lessons from a
REFORMED
KNUCKLEHEAD

Let me tell you a little more about my own background so you can see why this all has become so important to me. When I began writing this book, I considered this title instead: *Lessons from a Reformed Knucklehead.*

I was born in Chicago in 1963. My mother and father got a divorce when my sister and I were young, well before I went to kindergarten. My mother, Jan, raised us. It seems you never fully appreciate your parents until you have your own kids, and then you think, "Wow, this has come full circle. Isn't it amazing what they managed to do?" To appreciate something and to value something, you have to have some experience and context. Parents wonder why their children leave the lights on: "These kids just don't appreciate what it's like to have to pay the bills!" And it's true. Kids don't know any better. As parents and teachers and coaches, we sow what the children will one day reap. We plant, knowing we may not be there for the harvest.

I didn't spend time with my father, John, or even know him, until I was in my 30s. When we were children, he was out of contact with us, and yet my mother raised us, and we saw my grandparents and aunts and uncles on both sides. Later on, when we met, my father apologized for those years he was out of touch. He said he was sorry for the two innocent victims, meaning my sister and me. I told him that there was only one victim, and that was him, for having missed out. And I told him I had no idea what to call him. *Father* sounded too formal, and I'd never called him Dad. I didn't feel like calling him John. It's strange at 33 to meet somebody who looks just like you but whom you haven't known.

My mother had been everything to my sister, Jennifer, and me. We lived in an apartment in Chicago, where my mom was a secretary for Combined Insurance Company. One of her bosses was the renowned businessman, philanthropist, and new thought self-help author W. Clement Stone. I went to a Chicago public elementary school, Helen C. Pierce School, on the north side.

My grandparents were farmers and dairy people in northern Indiana, about 90 minutes from where we lived in Chicago. So we spent time in the city growing up, and then we spent time at the farm. My mom used to tell us we had the best of both worlds.

When it came time to go to high school, my mom had promised my grandmother, my father's mother, that she would do everything she could to make sure that our education was the best possible. She was a single parent on a secretary's income, and instead of sending me to a Chicago public high school she opted for Loyola Academy, a Jesuit college preparatory school for boys. It was in Wilmette, Illinois, about a 60-minute bus and train ride from home.

So I went from the Chicago public elementary school to this Catholic high school in a fairly affluent area. People there had plenty of resources. I felt as if I'd come in halfway through the movie. I didn't hate high school, but it was difficult for me every day. Chicago winters are cold. I stood each school morning on the elevated platform to take the train to school, shivering in temperatures that could drop to zero and below.

I found myself contemplating whether I really wanted to do this. I wasn't a bad kid. I was always into sports—basketball, at that time—and when I came home from school, I went straight outside every day. I was never in trouble, I never experimented with drugs or alcohol, and I never spent one minute in detention. But I wasn't engaged academically at all.

And then one June day at the end of my sophomore year, I got my report card, and it was straight Fs. I knew I wasn't doing well, but I didn't know I was getting straight Fs. It came to my home along with a letter saying I'd been kicked out and good luck.

"YOU'D BETTER FIX IT"

That letter tore my mother in two. Today, as a parent myself, I can imagine how much she was sacrificing on a modest income to send her son to a private, Catholic, all-boys high school. She had invested two years of hard work in our tuition. Where she got the resources, I don't know, but she probably spent a quarter or more of her take-home pay on that tuition for my sister and me. And I had screwed up. Her dream had been to provide this opportunity for me to grasp, and this was how I'd repaid her. She looked at me and said, "I don't know how this is going to get fixed, but you'd better fix it."

I went back to the school and was able to get a meeting with Mr. Graf, and Father Arimond, the headmaster. Mr. Graf asked me, simply, why this had happened. I don't remember what I said, but they let me back in—with some conditions. I had to go to summer school. I had to retake all the courses I'd failed. And I had to take a full load in my junior and senior years—no free periods.

I often tell students that "if they find themselves in a hole, they must put down the shovel." I went on to get grades good enough to graduate, but it was hard to offset that semester of straight Fs to even get to the required 2.0 cumulative GPA. So in my senior year, I was unable to play high-school sports because of the challenge I'd had academically, and because of how far I had to travel when the trains stopped running. In fact, I had a basketball coach there, named Coach Fitzgerald, and he would give me a ride home when I needed one, though it was way out of his way.

"IT'S AN HONOR TO BE CALLED COACH"

A coach came into my life at Loyola Academy named Coach Fred Wright, who was actually the athletic director, and he gave me a job at the summer camp so I could make some money along with daily encouragement and advice. The job experience Coach Wright was providing was merely the medium through which he would guide and mentor me.

One day Coach Frank Amato, the dean of students and track coach who was at one point the football coach, called me into his office and started talking to me about colleges. He was the first guy to tell me that he thought I'd make a good coach. As I write this, Coach Amato is 86 and will be retiring this year. Thanks to the impact these men had on my life, I knew that a coach is what I wanted to be and I made that known to everyone.

And then there was Coach Chuck Erlanbaugh, who was a football coach and a physical education teacher. I was in my senior year, and Coach Erlanbaugh, knowing I had to take a class every period, came to me and asked if I was interested in TAP, the teacher assistant program. I said sure, I'd love to do that.

He knew I was still overcoming all those Fs and didn't have a 2.0 yet, and still he offered me a chance to be in the teacher assistant program. Later, I asked him why he'd given me such a break.

"We know you want to be a coach someday," he said, "so we decided we were going to mentor you." He said, "we," so I knew he had conferred with the other coaches about what the plan was for me. These coaches helped me create a future that I hadn't envisioned, and was unable to envision, for myself. They invested in me, and I've always wanted to be like those men. Coach Amato is the one that told me that the term "COACH" is a term of endearment." "It's a title that you can never take lightly and one that you have to earn everyday. Remember John it's an honor to be called Coach" It is often said that every player deserves a coach that believes them. They believed in me and I am forever grateful. I feel their impact every day.

Coach Erlanbaugh awarded me an A in the TAP physical education program. It was my only A in high school, and it was the grade that got me over 2.0 so that I could graduate. I have learned that "a coach is a person that takes you where you are unable to take yourself." If you could take yourself there, you wouldn't need a coach. These men started

BAXTERISM

A coach is a person that takes you where you are unable to take yourself.

the process of taking me where I couldn't take myself. I am where I am today because of the start they gave me and the example they set.

WORDS THAT CHANGED MY LIFE

One day in 1981 when I was working as Coach Erlanbaugh's assistant—I basically did anything he needed done, such as fold gym towels, take roll, put the balls away or organize the intramural games—a coach named Bob Bierie came walking in. He was the Head Football Caoch at Loras College, a Catholic university in Dubuque, Iowa.

"Can you tell me where the football coach is?" he asked me.

"Sure, he's right over there," and I escorted him to see Coach Erlanbaugh. As we walked, he asked me who I was. I told him I was the teacher's assistant and wanted to be a coach. Later I got a phone call. It was Coach Bierie asking me if I'd like to come to school at Loras College. I told him it was certainly an interesting idea.

It was my practice to always consult with my coaches. I asked Coach Amato what he thought of the idea. He said it was something I needed to do, and Loras, a small Catholic school, would be a great place for me. So I called Coach Bierie back and said I'd like to take a closer look at the possibility of playing for him.

"I don't want you to play," he said. "I want you to coach." And those words changed my life.

I wasn't exactly quick to seize the opportunity. "You don't understand," I told him, "I want to play. I haven't been able to play Varsity sports because of travel logistics and grades and this is my chance to finally participate."

He explained that he'd just restarted a small Division 3 program and needed some help and that he would teach me to coach a position and help me get my career started early.

"Well, thanks, but that's not what I want right now," I told him.

I went back and told Coach Amato, and he gave me some clear directions. "You call him back," he told me, "and beg for that opportunity." And that's how I launched my career as a coach.

The two coaches at Loras College back then, Bob Bierie and Ralph Micheli, would become the next two important figures in my life. And they kept me in the channel. As a young adult in college, you do some things that you're proud of, and you make some errors in judgment because of your new found independence. They encouraged me daily, and they gave me some hard corrections when I needed them. There was no doubt about the standards and what their expectations were. Those standards did not compromise.

ROUGH START IN COLLEGE

Because my grades had been so weak in high school, Loras College accepted me on condition of what they called a one-semester review, which is academic probation. If I could attain a 2.0 at the end of the first semester, the condition would be lifted. During my first semester at school, everything seemed to be going great, at least as far as I was concerned. I was away at college and it was fun. I got three Cs and a D+. Those grades average 1.9. So I got the boot letter, right before Christmas vacation. I went to see Father Lang, the dean of students, who confirmed the rules.

"No, you don't understand," I told him. "There's no possible way I can go home and do this to my mother. There's no possible way this can happen. I need a second chance."

"You got a second chance. We admitted you on the second chance," he said.

"Then I need a third chance," I begged. He told me he would think about it and call me in a few days. In the meantime, I said nothing to my family. And sure enough, the phone rang.

"In early January," he said, "you will need to come back up here and appear before the Board of Readmissions. I want you to show us what it is you plan to do and do differently."

I started interviewing players on the team and asked how they studied. I made a three-ring binder with dividers and school supplies, and I included a free calendar that I got from a real estate office. I cut off the fishing scene and punched three holes in it. It was a comprehensive student organizer. And I talked to Pete Jebson, who was a place kicker on the team and who today is Dr. Peter J. Jebson, MD, an orthopedic surgeon in Michigan. He would write all his class scores on index cards. He told me he wanted to go to medical school and couldn't afford to get a B, so he needed to know where he stood in class at all times. BAM! Life changing!

So I followed Pete's lead and made a little score board out of graph paper for the binder. That same scoreboard concept is a fundamental part of Academic Gameplan to this day.

With binder in hand, I drove up to appear before the Board of Readmissions. I was punctual, and I wore nice clothes. I waited in the outer office, and finally, I was called in. The Academic Dean, Father Barta, was there, and the Director of Admissions, Dan Conry, and the registrar, Mr. Noonan. Father Lang was there too. This was thirty years ago, and I can see their faces now. They began to interview me. How comfortable did I feel in school? Did I feel that college was for me? I was asked an investigative question from one of the courses I had taken in the fall. I was asked "How was my family life?" And I was asked if I had a plan as to how I was going rectify my academic performance or lack there of. And then I pulled out my binder and passed it down the table. I could see them nodding as they examined it.

After a while, they asked me to wait in the outer office while they conferred. When they called me back in, they said, "We've reaccepted you."

As we were preparing to leave, Dan Conry turned to me and said, "By the way, Mr. Baxter, do you mind if I give you one piece of advice? You know this book you put together?"

"Yes," I said. "What about it?"

"Use it!"

The day after graduation, I went to the office to pick up my diploma, and I happened to see Dan Conry in the hallway of Keane Hall.

"I want to congratulate you," he said. "I remember how we were wondering whether to give you another chance, and, you know, you did all right."

"Yeah," I said. "Father Lang told me I had to appear before that Readmissions Board."

He looked at me. "I want to tell you something," he said. "That committee didn't exist. You're the only person we've ever readmitted."

CHAPTER 4

In the
REARVIEW
Mirror

"Use it," he had told me. He knew that the study binder I had created would be my source of college success if I just put it into practice. I did use it, and I do to this day. It helped me then, and it helps us now in Academic Gameplan.

The reason I wasn't doing well was an execution issue. It wasn't an intelligence issue. I was capable of remembering anything. I was capable of studying for a test. I was capable of writing a paper. What I wasn't capable of was multitasking, note taking, and strategic planning. I'd lacked a system of integrating notes with handouts, and preparing my own study guide. I didn't have the fundamentals. Once I got those skills in place, I was fine.

I think things often make sense in the rearview mirror. The trials and tribulations I've had in my own life, and in my own academic career, have had a lot to do with shaping what I do today. I was a good kid who didn't get in trouble, and yet my transcript was a mess, and that's how college admissions officers and others often judge us.

Low grades, however, aren't necessarily a reflection of intelligence. The problem for anyone who fails to perform well is mostly execution. How do you make the grade? The skills, and fundamentals critical to strategic planning and execution are not often taught, and that is what we are doing with Academic Gameplan.

In my years as a coach, I have met many students who fit that pattern of poor academic performance. I realized early on that it wasn't just a problem for football players; it was common in other sports. And it wasn't just a problem among athletes but among all students, and not just college students, high-school students too, and earlier. They don't have a clue how to play the game of school. They don't know how to execute in academia.

We've all heard of the so-called dumb jock. I choose to dispel that myth. It's a horrible stereotype and it's flat-out untrue. As we have grown in our awareness in education, we've become increasingly more aware of multiple forms of intelligences and various styles of learning. People are kinesthetic, or visual, or auditory learners, or some combination thereof, and research suggests there are other styles as well.

In 1986 I was hired as a graduate assistant coach at Iowa State University on Jim Criner's coaching staff, I was sitting as a brand-new college graduate at staff meetings, and the talk often turned to players who were struggling or underperforming academically. The discussions always started the same way, as they invariably seem to start whenever the subject is a student with poor grades: "Well, you know, he's a good kid, but…"

That was me. It felt as if they were talking about me, the good kid who got all those Fs one semester. I can tell you that it doesn't have anything to do with whether you're a good kid, or a nice kid. It has to do with execution. I had seen that in my own life. I had seen what coaches with wisdom could do for a young person like that.

"WHAT A CHANGE!"

My experience began to grow as a young professional. I was 22 years old with a teaching certificate, beginning my coaching career. I decided to pull some of the guys aside at Iowa State when I was a study hall monitor and start working with them. "Tell me a little bit about your struggle," I would say. "Tell me what you've got going on. Have you ever tried this? Have you ever tried that?" Fairly quickly, they started to perform better.

Young coaches had to rotate through study hall, which meant we sat there for two hours and looked at these kids looking at a book. They were just flat-out disengaged. I had no idea what they were doing. I just had to make sure they were there on time and didn't leave and kept quiet.

Without telling anyone what I was doing, I started to make contact with them. I offered them tips, and suggested they take each class syllabus and break it down onto a month-at-a-glance calendar. That way they would have one combined syllabus that would help them see priorities. Every day when I was the study hall monitor, I would teach them what I would call a mini-lesson. Sure enough, they started seeking me out. "Hey, Coach, what about this? Hey, Coach, can you help me with my math homework?" When it came to specific subjects, I would always refer them to their teacher or a tutor. But I was happy to offer basic help on getting a paper started, setting up an outline, getting organized, creating a things-to-do list, getting started earlier, not waiting until the last minute.

At the end of that semester, when the grades came out, the head coach praised the other coaches on what a great job they had done with the players. "Those guys didn't even talk to the kids!" I thought, but nobody knew and I wasn't saying anything. That was the beginning of what has become my lifelong commitment to helping others avoid the pain that I went through academically. Today I'm saying plenty. I want to spread the word far and wide.

I went from Iowa State University in 1986 and '87 to the University of Arizona in '88 and the University of Maine in 1989 where I worked under the Director of Athletics Dr. Kevin White and Head coach Tom Lichtenberg. That was my first full-time job and for 30 years Dr. White has been a source of constant support. He is the consummate athletic administrator and greatest mentor to young coaches on administrators in the profession

We were an under-budgeted, small program at the University of Maine. We didn't have money for academic services. That's when I first officially put together some of these lessons that we now call Academic Gameplan—and our players did fantastically well. People were saying to our football staff, "What a change! These kids are doing so well."

I was only there one year before being hired back to the University of Arizona by Coach Dick Tomey. To this day I am grateful to every head coach that has offered me employment. I am forever thankful to Coach Tomey for his belief in me because he hired me at 26 as a full time coach in the PAC 10 conference. As a very young coach he had more confidence in me that I can say that I had in myself. He hired me to do a big job. At the time, we were having some academic struggles as most college athletic departments do.

I went to Coach Tomey, who had no idea that I'd been working on this academic plan, and said, "Coach, I've got an idea how we can help the players." We started a program. Sure enough, at the end of the year we had our highest freshman GPA in the history of the school. I was at the University of Arizona for two years. In 1992 I went to the University of Maryland and saw a similar issue. We started the program there, and again we had the highest GPA ever.

That's when I started to realize, the lack of good study habits has nothing to do with football. It has everything to do with students. Football players just happen to be the students I come in contact with. Students of any discipline need the same thing: a strong foundation and simple execution of rules, fundamentals, and techniques.

THINKERS, COMMUNICATORS, AND COMPETITORS

Year after year, we see students who don't know how to study, and the problem seems to show itself in about the seventh grade. Until then, most kids have one teacher throughout the school day. Middle school, or junior high, is the first time that students experience "interdisciplinary education," a fancy way to say that the students move and the teachers stay put. That's the first level where young people need that mastery of the fundamentals so they can execute on a variety of subjects. And that's where Academic Gameplan can intervene to lead them to success.

When most people hear about our program, they think of little Johnny or Joanie who is getting bad grades and how great it would be for them. Let me make this clear: This is for all students. None of us comes out of the womb knowing how to make a strategic plan. We don't know how to organize, or prepare for tests. We cannot anticipate, so it's hard to prepare.

Fundamentals are for everyone. The better you are at the fundamentals, the better you will play in the game. A student might get along for a while without mastering them because the subject matter is simple. Later, however, without a solid foundation, that student will be in trouble as the subjects become more diverse and complex. Just because a student is doing well now doesn't mean he or she will continue to do well as the complexities and academic pressures build. Students need the skills for success.

I wrote a philosophy statement for Academic Gameplan, and I present it as a question at the advanced levels: "Who are you, and what do you represent?" If I ask that question, I need to have an answer, and so I make clear to my students from the start that I'm there to turn them into thinkers, competitors, and communicators. When I talk to football players, in an all-male environment, I tell them they need to be "a man for others," to make the most of themselves so they can serve well.

Here's the document that I use to outline those principles for my players:

3 THINGS I WANT MY PLAYERS TO BE:

By Coach John Baxter (©Academic Gameplan 1999)

THINKERS, COMMUNICATORS, COMPETITORS AND A MAN FOR OTHERS

1. THINKER

    Your brain is your number 1 tool. Our ability to reason is what separates us from all other species. Thinking is the simple process of asking questions and finding answers. Successful people simply ask better questions. Successful people examine their options and use their resources to the fullest extent. Problem solving is the most valuable asset anyone can bring to any organization.

2. COMMUNICATOR

    Communication is how we interact with and learn about the world around us. It's also how we avoid misunderstandings and conflicts. "Conflict is merely an opportunity to communicate in disguise." It's okay to not understand, but it's not okay to not understand and not ask a question. The ability to express oneself accurately, effectively and succinctly is a major determining factor in ultimate success.

3. COMPETITOR

    As technology accelerates, so does technique. As technique improves, so does the competition. Technology breeds technique. Technology, simply explained, is a new and improved idea or application of resources. You'll be an athlete for part of your life, but to achieve true competitive greatness, you'll be a student your entire life! A student is simply someone who thinks, communicates, and competes, seeking competitive greatness in anything!

AND "A MAN FOR OTHERS"

Truly successful people live their life with an "attitude of gratitude." We are given talents and abilities, and they are for the express purpose of being shared, not buried. The greatest tragedy in life is unrealized potential due to injury, death, not getting an opportunity, or, worst of all, lack of effort, because that's the only one you can control. The law of reciprocation is absolute in that whatever emanates from you comes back to you from the world around you. The greatest gift is the gift of giving. Never underestimate the power of your influence!

> **BAXTERISM**
>
> Truly successful people live their life with an "attitude of gratitude."

AND DO IT WITH INTEGRITY

Integrity comes from the Latin integrits, meaning "soundness," "whole," or "complete." Integrity is related to the word integer. An integer is a whole number. Integrity has to do with wholeness or completeness of performance. The quality or condition of being whole or undivided; completeness. A person is an indivisible whole, and what shows up in one area of performance usually is a consistent trait throughout that person's performance, regardless of the situation. Integrity has to do with working toward similar standards of performance and quality in all areas and phases of life.

First and foremost, I help young people be thinkers, which basically means problem solvers. In any business and industry, problem solving is a valuable skill, and it requires thinking. It also requires communicating, because we cannot go through life alone. "Life is a team sport." If you want something or need something, you have to ask for it. When I

BAXTERISM

Life is a team sport.

had to appeal for another chance to stay in school, if I hadn't communicated, I would have been kicked out. If I had just gnawed at my fingernails, nothing would have happened.

You have to learn to compete in life, as you do in sports. If you want something, you have to go get it. You're either going to be predator or you're going to be prey. In this country and in this economy opportunity is everywhere. But you've got to go out and grasp it and compete for it.

One of the things that I tell young people early on, in our relationship as a player and a coach, is that if football is the only thing I ever talk to them about, we've wasted our time. Everything we do together, every day, must involve thinking, communicating, and competing, whether it has to do with school, or football, or anything else.

ATTITUDE FIRST

I think of the "Parable of the Talents" in Matthew 25. A man was heading out on a journey and entrusted his gold to three servants, each according to his abilities. To one he gave five bags, to the second he gave two, and to the third he gave one. The first two servants doubled the gold by putting it to work, but the third servant buried the bag entrusted to him. When the man returned, he put the first two servants in charge of many of his affairs, but he banished the third servant. The first two servants had an attitude of abundance, but the third had an attitude of fear.

That's where the Jesuit training comes out in me. You are taught about living your life with an attitude of gratitude, being appreciative for what comes to you, and always looking to help other people in need.

Many books have been written on study skills, but Academic Gameplan goes far deeper. It gets down to the attitudes that form the foundation of learning. We identify those rules, fundamentals, and techniques and help students apply them for success. Our society has slowly been reaching the point where education is considered the right of every child. Yet we take that for granted. That must stop. Until we break through the attitudes and get down to the fundamental reasons behind the lack of execution, a book about study habits will have limited value. The attitude problem underlies the skills problem. You cannot plant a seed and expect it to grow when the soil is toxic.

IN RETROSPECT

As I look into that rearview mirror and think about my own experiences in school and as a coach and teacher, I am thankful for the many lessons I have learned. As a student, I discovered the hard way that one must execute if one is to succeed. I had ability, and I finally learned to use it. I changed my attitude and began to focus on thinking, communicating, and competing. As a coach, I soon found a way to help others avoid the pain that I had experienced by sharing with them what I had learned. I became a man for others.

It is my fervent hope that those I have touched in my coaching career will look into their own rearview mirrors and see what they have gained and then steer a straight course forward, helping others to gain the same.

— CLINT'S FIELD NOTE —

I came from a successful entrepreneurial family. Excellence was expected. In high school I scratched and clawed my way and managed to get As and Bs, but with massive frustration. I wasn't in control. I wasn't a great problem solver. I just persevered to stay out of trouble with my parents, particularly my mom.

I found a way to do all right in school, but that doesn't mean that I wasn't in great need of skill development and coaching. A lot of people don't have the kind of parents that I did, who put leadership before friendship. I wasn't given a choice not to do well. Other guys, who lacked skills and didn't have anyone demanding they perform, just didn't bother. Either way, nobody was teaching the fundamental skills so that excellence continues for a lifetime, long after the parents are out of the picture. I saw the pattern in a lot of my teammates over the years. I heard the same stories in NFL locker rooms. East Coast or West Coast, urban or rural, no matter the socioeconomic background, or race, or ethnicity, I saw the same cross-section of core beliefs and attitudes.

When Coach Baxter left my house after his recruiting visit with me and my father, I felt a resolve to prove what I could be—and that was the very best. Regardless of any evaluation, I knew who I was and where I was going. I was on a mission to prove myself. But I'm coachable. If someone with expertise tells me where I'm lacking and what I need to do, I'll just do it.

I'd been a big fish in a small pond. I had boxes of marketing materials on schools in every conference. Wisconsin, LSU, Louisville, Cal, Arizona State. I was getting plenty of praise in the newspapers. When a young person is recruited, he's expecting a coach to come in and tell him how much he's needed and how limitless his future is. That's what I thought I'd hear. And the athletes' parents are excited too; my dad was as proud of me and as excited as anyone. What you do not expect is to hear that you have a long way to go and here's how to get there. Coach felt I could become the kicker I needed to become, but I wasn't there yet, and he knew I needed to hear that.

Later, at the team's first meeting with Coach Baxter, we got our binders and planners. He taught us to break stuff down, prioritize, and read efficiently. I'm a slow reader. I comprehend what I read, but I'm slow. And as we learned his teaching methods, I felt freedom. I had known who I wanted to be, but I had been held back by not knowing how to do it. I had done all right through persistence. I was in a constant cage of stress and just worked through it, as I had no other choice. I met with him, and I was given freedom. I knew how to take control of my life. I knew how to take control of things that had debilitated me because I knew how much time and effort they'd take. I learned to accomplish major things with small, constant repetitions. I learned to organize, and I learned to anticipate.

How can you know the answers if you don't know the questions? Some of the guys were like me in that they had the right background and just needed to get over the hump of the techniques and the tools. But other guys didn't even know there was a question. They had no clue about school, no foundation. No one told them otherwise, other than their football coaches and those who warned them to pay attention so they would remain eligible.

It's not that they didn't want to care. They didn't know how to care. No one told them how or why. They considered studying to be uncool. No one took the time to give them a reason or a way to understand it. Nobody showed them responsibility and accountability.

Academic Gameplan took some of us to the next level, but it gave others the very foundation and showed them, for the first time, a direction. My father-in-law says it best. I had a couple of friends who didn't seem to be doing much except partying after graduating from college. "They're just living without a purpose," he observed. "They're just out there, floating in the universe." That's what some of my teammates seemed to be doing. They were just out there. They had no direction at all. The program showed them the way.

I remember some of those guys speaking at graduation. They had been given no hope, no chance, by so many in their lives, even their high-school counselors and principals. They had been labeled as academically hopeless and written off. Today they are college graduates and good family men with careers, doing well in life. But high school failed them. They never got the skills there that they needed.

CHAPTER 5

School
DAZE

On the stage at a seminar, I hold up a crisp twenty-dollar bill for all to see. I crumple it up. I pour a cup of water over it and toss it to the floor, step on it, and grind it with my shoe. Then I kick it off the stage.

People dive out of their chairs for that bill as if it were candy tossed from a parade float. I've turned it into a filthy, sodden mess, ragged and torn, and yet they fly from their chairs to get to it first. I tell whoever manages to grab it that he or she can keep it, but first, I have a few questions for that person.

"What did you just do?" I ask.

"I picked up a twenty-dollar bill."

"Why?"

"Well, because it's twenty bucks. You know. I can buy stuff with it."

"But why did you pick it up?" I persist. Eventually I hear the fundamental reason: "It has value."

"Value?"

"Sure."

"So, regardless of how it has been treated, it has value," I point out. "Even though I crumpled and abused it and kicked it aside, it's worth something."

I look out over the audience. "And let me ask you this: Don't all those young people who are struggling, who have been kicked around by people or by life, have value, too? Just because of who they are?"

BECAUSE THAT'S WHAT WE DO

Starting in kindergarten and for years thereafter, we all go to school. Why? Because that's what we do—and therein lies the problem. We go there because that's where we go, and we do what we do there. At no point does the system of education stop the assembly line and say, "This is why we're here, and this is why we're doing this."

When I talk with teachers, I hear recurring themes, and by far the top frustration that they express is that kids don't seem to be able to think past the end of their noses. They don't think long-term. But in truth, the teachers and the educational system are producing the problem. As a father of high-school kids, I see what is happening.

The Department of Agriculture at Fresno had an issue similar to that of the athletic department. There are only so many ag students, and if a school wants to have an exemplary department, it has to recruit them and make sure they stay. Ag schools compete for students, unlike business or education or other popular university departments that always have plenty of applicants. The department head asked me to show Academic Gameplan to the faculty, and so I gave them a presentation.

"Coach, this is a really interesting discussion," one of the professors said. "But I'm thinking the students should come here already with these types of skills. That's not my job to teach these things."

"Well," I replied, "if I accept that at face value, then let me ask you this: Whose job was it? Who was officially in charge of teaching it to them?"

There was a pause. "That's not the point," he said. "It's not for me to know."

"You're right," I said. "It's not for me to know, either. Because nobody does it." Everyone passes off the responsibility, and when the problem reaches the college level, we say that somebody else should have taught it. The professors have the attitude that they teach biology, or chemistry, or physics, and that it's just not their job to teach the basics of good study habits.

That's an attitude that began back in the middle and high schools. I recently did an in-service day for the faculty of a high school at the invitation of the principal, who is a friend of mine. The fact that I get such requests shows how much our program has grown in the years since I helped a few disenfranchised students in a back room at Iowa State. I explained to the faculty that students should take the syllabus for each of their subjects and break them down and combine them into a long-term strategic plan.

"You have a syllabus for every subject, right?" I said. They all assured me that they did, but then the principal raised his hand, and he looked chagrined. "Coach, hold on a second," he said. "I have to tell you something. About having a syllabus for every class, well, we do, but we've actually never thought about giving them to the students."

"Then, what's the point?" I asked.

"The state requires it," he explained. "We create a syllabus so that we hit the timelines on the curriculum. But that's for the teachers, so that they all get the material covered."

"Tell me this, then," I said. "How do the students know how to prepare for a test that's coming up in two weeks, or, when to get started on a paper?"

The teachers started chiming in, explaining that each day they wrote on the board the exercises they would do in class that day and the homework for that night. The students were supposed to write it all down in their planners.

"They have planners? When do you issue those?" I asked.

"At the beginning of the school year."

"How much time have you spent teaching them how to use the planners?"

"We don't do that. They should know how to use them."

"So let me get this straight," I said. "You're telling each student what to do in class today and what's due tomorrow. Your system doesn't tell them anything's due more than a day ahead of time. And your biggest frustration is that students don't seem to be able to think beyond the end of their noses? What do you expect? You're not encouraging long-term planning. You're the problem, not the kids."

Teachers and parents alike say they want to instill independence in young people, and yet they create a dependent environment. That's what a "helicopter parent" does, the kind that hovers over all their kids' activities and decisions. And that's what teachers do when they spoon-feed the students. A syllabus would help the students think long-term. And if teachers think the students would just misplace it or forget it, that's also breeding dependence. It's saying they don't believe in the kids.

FOUR REASONS FOR POOR GRADES

There's a void in American education. Students are falling through cracks in the system, and those cracks grow wider because so many students lack study skills and techniques. Back in 1997, when I wrote Academic Gameplan, the overall high-school dropout rate was 4.7 percent. In addition, 35 percent of all high-school graduates stopped their education there and didn't attend college. Far fewer than half of those who enter school ultimately get a college degree. The numbers are startling.

Here's why, once again: Nobody teaches students how to study. That's the major reason that they don't get good grades. They become disinterested, and disenfranchised, and they drop out. They become like that crumpled twenty-dollar bill on the floor, but nobody rushes to pick them up. It's high time we saw the value in all our young people. It's critical that we ask why this is happening. There are four primary reasons for poor grades:

> **Teachers teach subjects, not skills.** Again, their attitude is this: "I'm the biology teacher (or the chemistry, math, history, you-name-it teacher), and my job is to teach biology, not study skills." Why don't students think beyond the end of their nose? Because the teacher doesn't think beyond the end of his or her own nose. The gap begins in middle school, when the student no longer has just one teacher. Now, he or she goes through the day seeing first one teacher and then another, then a coach after school, before going home. Nobody seems to be connecting the dots. The teachers in the higher grades don't see the whole child the same way the fourth-grade teacher saw that

child. Kids who haven't mastered the fundamentals and techniques start to fall behind.

» **Some teachers simply don't teach well.** Think about the number of influential teachers you have had. Most people say they could count them on one hand. Most are ineffectual or unmemorable, and that, to me, is sad. Teachers in the audience at my seminars don't like to hear that. "Don't get mad," I tell them. "I'm one of you. I'm an educator, not some outsider pointing out the problem. I'm on the inside of this battle." Instructors at the highest levels in college can teach without ever having taken a course in how to do it. They just need their doctorate or whatever qualifies them to be the expert in their topic. They have whatever certifies them to be teachers, and they exchange a lot of information. But few of them are able to dig into the souls of the kids in their classrooms and engage them, and they can't really get a handle on how much the students understand. The teachers don't know the level of rookie they're dealing with.

» **Parents are not involved enough.** Often the household has a single parent who has to work and comes home dead tired, or both parents have to work to make ends meet in today's economy. For whatever reason, many parents simply are uninvolved in their children's education. Yet even the most involved parent doesn't sit in class daily with the student. And so the conversations are predictable: "What'd you do in school today?" "Nothing." "How much homework do you have?" "None." And they don't. Or perhaps they know there's nothing due tomorrow that was assigned today, because that's the extent of the "strategic" planning on the educational assembly line.

» **Students don't know how or why to be a student.** The kids need a higher level of organization and skills. The teachers, focused on their subjects, don't instill those skills, and the kids start to slide. They don't know how to take notes. They don't know how to study. They don't know strategies for taking tests. If they learn what works, it's through trial and error. But when people start encountering error after error, the human tendency is to start to give up. The more frustration they experience, the less they want to try.

Together, those are the four ingredients in a recipe for disaster. The fact that anybody can make good grades is amazing.

People make a big deal about how many times Lincoln ran for office or how many attempts Edison made to develop the light bulb. You are talking about highly motivated people who weren't going to take no for an answer. What happens to people who feel far less motivated and lack a burning desire and even a reason for being in school? They'll try a couple of times. Somebody will yell at them, tell them they're an idiot, and they will never try again.

In the winner's vocabulary, the word try doesn't exist. The word is do. "Trying is simply losing with honor." "Oh, I tried." That's not a reason for not having

BAXTERISM

Trying is simply losing with honor.

finished your homework. That just means you're losing with honor. "I tried" assumes that when you hit an impasse, you did look for help. The problem is you didn't hit the impasse until the night before the assignment was due because it wasn't given to you until the day before.

THE VICIOUS CIRCLE

The mechanics of losing, assuming one has the TALENT & RESOURCES!

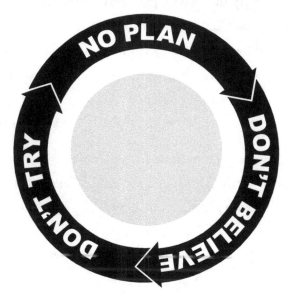

THE "VICIOUS CIRCLE"

When I ask my players what impacted them the most in Academic Gameplan, invariably they mention "the vicious circle." The vicious circle illustrates the three reasons for lack of success. It shows the mechanics of losing, and it's important to know about that before we can ever learn how to win. Life is a game that holds many rewards for those who dare to compete. Winning is never an accident, and neither is losing. The key to success is knowing the rules, techniques, and fundamentals of the game and having a plan for attaining the goal. That plan could have a multitude of forms; it doesn't matter what the plan is as long as you have one.

Have you ever seen a talented team lose? Of course you have, and it doesn't really matter what reason you give for that loss. If the issue were presented in the style of a political cartoon, all those reasons would be raindrops, and they would all fall into a bucket. On the bucket would be written the words, "Didn't execute." No matter how many reasons you come up with, or how many excuses, a talented team loses because it doesn't execute. The team members don't follow through on what they know they need to do. Something escapes them, a rule, a technique, a fundamental of some sort.

The next question is this: "Did you ever see an intelligent kid make a low grade?" Obviously, it happens, and again, you could come up with many reasons to excuse those low grades, but the reason an intelligent kid falls short is lack of execution. Many students don't know what, when, why, or how to execute. If they did, more of them would.

The vicious circle has three elements: You don't believe. You don't try. You have no plan. That's why people who otherwise have talent and resources end up losing. Most people have talent and resources that they could tap.

The most vicious part of that circle is "don't believe." When I taught Academic Gameplan before the season of 2011, I handed out note cards to the team and asked all the players to write down their name and their prediction for our win-loss record that year. We were playing 12 games. After they wrote those two numbers, I asked them to identify which games we wouldn't win. I collected the note cards and read the names and the games that each player expected to lose. "Player X, we're leaving you behind when we go to Oregon and Notre Dame," I announced, and "Player Y, you're not going to Stanford."

I could see by the looks on their faces that I'd made my point: If you don't believe, don't get on the bus. If you don't believe you can win, there is no point in even starting the game. Those guys still talk about that to this day.

The role of the teacher is always and forever to build a big enough why, to generate curiosity and belief on the part of the student. I showed them the vicious circle. When you look at teams that have the necessary talent but underachieve, often the reason is that the players don't believe. It's the same in academics: Many students walk into school every day believing they can't do it. And they don't. If you don't believe, you're far less likely to even try, and you're not going to be coming up with a plan.

I have never felt crumpled and kicked like that twenty dollar bill on the floor. Even when I was a student making terrible grades, I never questioned whether I had value. I knew that I did. I believed in me, and that's why I had the initiative to come up with a plan to lift myself out of that mess. I believed, I tried, I planned. My family had instilled in me a sense of value. I had some coaches who saw the best in me and told me, "You could be really good at that."

That's all it takes. And when you see a twenty-dollar bill lying all crumpled and torn on the floor, just pick it up and smooth it out and take it to the bank. Every player deserves a coach who believes in him.

WHO PREPARES THE STUDENT?

In elementary school, as I've pointed out, the teacher sees the same students throughout the day, and therefore is more likely to be in touch with an individual's strengths and struggles. The teacher may recognize whether a student is having problems at home, or isn't eating properly, or is having emotional difficulties. The teacher sees the whole person. In middle school, the teachers just see a piece of the person, for less than an hour a day.

It's in middle school where a student will begin to slip severely if he or she is lacking in technique, and in this day of technological savvy, we're doing the worst job in history of teaching technique. In middle school and beyond, the student has advanced beyond the grade school fundamentals of reading, writing, and arithmetic. Strategic planning is essential, and it's not being taught. Instead, the student is ushered through from period to period, week to week, semester to semester, year to year.

When a student begins performing poorly in class, the so-called educators often respond in knee-jerk fashion. The student may be assigned to study hall, which is sort of an academic prison. They go there because they lack the fundamentals, but they still lack them, and so their frustration grows. They may start to behave badly as a result.

When the parents notice those poor grades, they may have another knee-jerk reaction, with the best of intentions. They hire a tutor. This is common in high schools and certainly in colleges, particularly in athletic departments. The idea is to get the student to spend time with an expert on the subject. That's like putting a Band-Aid on cancer. The low grade might not be due to an inability to understand the subject, and therefore the tutor isn't the answer. If a student is having trouble in math or English or across the board, the problem might lie in other struggles that he or she is going through. The problem might be social or emotional; it might be economic; it might be nutritional; or it might be a lack of technique and under-standing of strategic planning. Maybe the kid just needs to learn how to build a study guide. Even if the tutor helps the student get a higher grade in a subject, the underlying cause might remain unaddressed. It's just treating the symptoms.

MEDICATING THE PROBLEM

I'll be blunt. I believe in teaching technique, not dispensing medication. We have created an overmedicated society, in which drugs are prescribed unnecessarily, and I find that particularly distressing in regard to treating children for diagnoses such as ADD, ADHD, and some other conditions that are believed to be the source of learning difficulties.

I'm not denying that those conditions exist. Research has given us insights that we didn't have just a few decades ago. But this reliance on medication to solve the issues of students making low grades is insanity to me. I don't even buy the term *learning disability*. As I see it, if you ask the question, "Can this person learn?" and the answer is yes, there is no disability. There's just a difference. I don't believe in learning disabilities, I believe in learning differences.

BAXTERISM

I don't believe in learning disabilities, I believe in learning differences.

Maybe a student doesn't learn at the same pace as someone else, and that's okay. Education is a matter of individualized teaching. Maybe someone learns in a different manner than others, and that's fine. But I don't think it's ever a good idea to suggest to someone that he or she is disabled, or unable. One thing I've learned from thirty years of coaching is that if you give a kid an excuse to lose, he will lose. Competitive greatness does not arise from labeling someone as disabled.

I think that often what is happening is that helicopter parents are looking for a reason to explain their children's poor grades. And so they go to the medical doctor. And sure enough, the doctor comes up with the diagnosis and the prescription and the label. I think we need to recognize that. There are, of course, some young people who truly have perceptual or processing differences and may need treatment but not nearly at the level at which society today is diagnosing and medicating.

CHANGE BEGINS AT THE EDGES

I believe strongly that most learning problems can be resolved without pills or tutors or shuffling a kid off to study hall. My own thoughts on the matter began to gel when I read a book by Joel Arthur Barker called *Paradigms: The Business of Discovering the Future.* I had felt as if I were alone in my beliefs about our educational system, and the book led me to realize that's where change begins. When a paradigm shifts, Barker says, it usually shifts at the edges. It shifts at the periphery. It shifts with people who are not currently part of the dominant thought. You need courage to be in that position, because people will call you crazy. When Galileo presented the idea that the sun was the center of the universe, he was almost put to death for heresy. But he held on to what he knew to be true.

In the late 1960s the country that led the world in watch making was Switzerland, with well over 90 percent market share. The Japanese share in the industry was just a few percent. And yet ten years later, Japan led the world in watch making. The technological change that revolutionized the industry was the quartz movement. The Swiss produced the first quartz wristwatch, but their paradigm disapproved of a battery-powered watch for commercial production.

They felt it would cheapen the watch as a work of art. The Japanese, however, felt it would cheapen the watch—that is, lower the production cost so that they could make ten for the price of one. And the watch would have no spring to break, wouldn't need to be wound, and would be far more accurate. It was a paradigm shift that shook the watch-making industry.

As a paradigm shift in education, why is it that a college football coach is offering reform? You would not think that that's where it would originate, but think of it this way: If too many athletes fail history and English and become ineligible to compete, it's not the history and English teachers who will lose their jobs. But the football coach might be gone at the end of the season.

Coaching is higher education's version of merit pay. You win, you stay. You lose, you're gone. That's how it is. The young athlete's performance influences the coach's livelihood, and so the coach is concerned not only with how the athlete does on the field, but also with how he does in the classroom, and how he behaves in social settings. If he gets in trouble, they call the coach. If he acts out in class or underperforms, they call the coach. And if we don't win the games, they call the coach.

This leads you very quickly to a fork in the road. We can bend the rules for these young people and manipulate the system so that they can get through and stay eligible, or we can invest deeply in them and help them technically and fundamentally so that they can become legitimate, independent performers.

I see myself at the center of the paradigm change. Study halls and medication and other quick fixes aren't what we need. They aren't the long-term solution. We need sustained, fundamental change. The change is not likely to come from the classroom teacher. The people who see these kids three days a week for 50 minutes or two days a week for 90 minutes and then may never see them again aren't the people who are going to be able to effect long-term change in those children's lives. They don't have enough contact with them. As a coach, I have an opportunity that teachers do not.

And when I speak, coaches listen. They're the first whose antennas go up. Why? Because they deal with eligibility every single day. If an English teacher or a math teacher or a science teacher has a young person failing their subject, he or she merely fails the subject. If the child fails too many subjects, he may be out, whether dropped out, or kicked out, or placed in an alternative curriculum. The teacher stays on the assembly line. But if too many athletes fall by the wayside, the coach doesn't have a team, which means he doesn't have a job.

When I speak to a group of principals, they often urge me to talk to the teachers who really need to hear it. The teachers urge me to talk to the counselors who really need to hear it. The counselors urge me to talk to the principals and teachers. Everyone passes the buck without taking action. The teachers stick to their subject and anything else just isn't their job.

If we are going to effect permanent, long-lasting, fundamental change, it is going to have to happen as a paradigm shift that begins somewhere other than in the schools. Then the schools will have to embrace it. Until then, parents will need to pursue such change individually through a program such as Academic Gameplan.

WHAT THE TESTS CANNOT MEASURE

"No Child Left Behind" is just a political slogan. It is a statement without substance. It sounds good, resonates, and gets politicians elected, but it doesn't lead to change. It was designed to test kids and get them up to a prescribed level of achievement. That's called high-stakes testing. It creates such a focus on the test that anything that is not on it no longer has a place in school. If a topic is not on the standardized tests, it's not included in the curriculum. There goes drama; there goes dance; there goes metal shop; there goes wood shop; there goes music; there goes physical education; there goes athletics.

It is a sad situation, because in those "extracurricular" activities, students often are able to really figure out who they are as a person, as a learner, as a competitor. They learn to think not just with the logical left side of the brain but also with the intuitive and creative right side. Colleges offer BA degrees and BS degrees because our world is divided into art or science and we need both. Consider the automobile. The mechanics are science, but the body style is art. Achievement in the arts is not easy to put on a test. As a coach, I teach the left brain, with the skills and the plays and demonstrations. But once the players go out on the grass, everything is art after the quarterback says "hike."

When you watch a great running back, a great quarterback, a great receiver, a great basketball player, a great musician, a great dancer, or a great salesman, you are beholding art. The way in which people solve problems is an art, not science. But that's what is being cut from curriculums at a record pace. And I, for one, am unwilling to accept it.

— CLINT'S FIELD NOTE —

Why is it that consumers always seem to be demanding their money's worth, except when it comes to education? Coach Baxter points that out repeatedly to his players. If they paid to go to a movie, he says, they'd throw a fit if the theater staff told everyone to go home because they didn't feel like showing the movie that day. Why then are the players happy if a teacher cancels class? Coach's point is that we need to demand our money's worth, and that the teachers and coaches and administrators and counselors work for the students. It might seem as if it's the other way around. After all, the teachers give out assignments. But we need a paradigm shift in which we start demanding from education what we want from it.

As a student, I became a buyer of my own education. I decided to make the most of it. One must assume that responsibility. As the coaching staff often said, "Every time you point a finger at somebody else, you'll find three fingers pointing back at you." And those were more than just words. It's easy to tell someone to stop blaming all the external circumstances in life and to take ownership and control. Students hear words like that, but nobody follows up with "Here's how to do it."

Most parents tell their children that education matters and that they need to prepare now for a prosperous future. I love and appreciate my parents, and they certainly made that point, but for years I felt as if I were doing it for them, not myself. I was working hard to pacify others, to let everyone know I was doing what I'd been told I was supposed to do. For me, the breakthrough came through Coach Baxter. He was going to show me exactly how to maximize my purchase. As athletes, we became buyers of knowledge and skills for ourselves, and that awakening was backed by the techniques we needed to make that happen. Out of that, our confidence grew.

That's what it takes. Even if parents were to offer all the technical details, their children would tend not to hear it very well until someone pulled them aside to say, "Listen up! Your parents are right, and here's why." Maybe it's an older brother or sister, maybe a neighbor, or maybe a coach.

Athletes who play for Coach Baxter are among the top 1 percent in the sport, and in the beginning of their career they're not always known for great academics, and yet they uniformly praise a guy who puts academics first. If you see that others believe in him, you're going to believe in him yourself. You're going to follow his advice to demand your money's worth, and with him, you're certainly going to get it.

CHAPTER 6

The Magic of WHY

"We waste education on the young." I remember those words to this day. I heard them in 1995 during a homily at a mass in New Orleans, where Reverend Monsignor Ignatius Roppolo was talking about continuing education. Eighteen years later, those words resonate with me. I believe that it's not so much that we waste education on the young but that they don't appreciate the educational process.

Such appreciation arises from experience, and you have to be taught to appreciate things. We come to understand our parents and what they have done, for example, as the years go by and when we have our own children. We tell our children the same thing our parents told us: "Someday, you'll appreciate this." The circle of life continues as we feel the gratitude.

By definition, young people are in school because they don't know about the topic or subject. They lack experience and maturity. That's what they are there to gain, and, with life experience, they will come to value it. Some day.

They will be slowed down, however, unless our schools do a better job of helping them understand their why. That's one of the building blocks of Academic Gameplan. The other is understanding the power of how, as we will explore in the next chapter. Together, those are the secret to good coaching, good teaching, good parenting and good business. In fact, those are the building blocks to success in life.

The most basic question that any person asks is "Why?" Toddlers ask it incessantly. "Mommy, why is the sky blue? Why is the grass green?" It can frustrate and irritate parents to the point where they say, "Don't ask so many questions!" And that's an insane response. Those questions reflect the development of critical thinking.

When my daughters, Kelly and McKenzie, were little, they would see me heading off to work most days—seven days a week, for seven months. And they'd see me coming home later. They accepted that, but then one day they asked me, "Where did you go?" I told them I went to work. "What's work?" they asked. There comes a time in their development when children no longer are willing to just accept their surroundings at face value. They want to know the why behind it all. Too often, adults stifle that natural impulse rather than embrace the growth of intellect. And later, they're upset when young people cannot seem to solve problems. It takes critical thinking to solve problems, and that has to be nurtured. Instead, adults often crush it in young people.

The number-one job of a teacher is to inspire future learning. If you can do that, you've done your job. Getting from A to Z in a subject is not inspiring future learning. That's just thumbing through the textbook. True education requires pulling the students in, engaging them,

BAXTERISM

The number-one job of a teacher is to inspire future learning.

putting issues out there, giving them problems to think through. That's how you teach the magic of why, and that's how we address it in Academic Gameplan.

If I were in charge of the schools, every classroom would be a laboratory for reading, strategic planning, and problem solving. Every course, including physical education, would involve a writing component because writing crystallizes thinking. I would insist on some level of written communication, regardless of the subject, and each teacher would be required to build a big enough why for these being the central requirements. The "Magic of Why" and the "Power of How," which this section is devoted to, are the major building blocks upon which I have built this entire AGP program. If at any point you would like to learn more, you are always welcome to visit us at AGP101.com.*

BAXTERISM

The "Magic of Why" and the "Power of How."

A QUESTION FOR ALL TEACHERS

One day I was in the office of Jeff Eben, a principal who is one of my best friends. He was building a new school and putting together his initial administrative team and his learning directors. They had been discussing the direction of the new school, which had no template or students yet. They were talking about the subjects to be taught and how its departments would function. Jeff was telling me about the interviews he was conducting to find the best teachers and personnel.

I told him I knew a great way to do that, and it would take about five minutes per person. "I want you to call in every teacher

---

*   *See page 175 for a special offer.*

you're interviewing," I said, "and ask him or her one fundamental question. If it's an algebra teacher, for instance, ask: "Why is algebra so important that it must stay in the curriculum, and why should you be the instructor? Do the same with the history, biology, and chemistry teachers. And if they are unable answer the question, they don't get hired." It has been a long-standing belief of mine that the teacher works for the student; the student does not work for the teacher. The hiring process should select people who represent this value. Remember, you get what you bait your hook for!

That was another way of making my point: Any teacher who is going to inspire future learning must build a big enough why. Then the child will naturally seek the how. Think about it: What is marketing and advertising? You're building a big enough why for your product and then people naturally seek the how, as in: how do they get the product? Even though this is a fundamental of marketing and business, we've lost our focus on it as the number-one job of a teacher.

A young person should hear something like this on the first day of class: "I am Mr. Jones, and this is freshman Algebra I, and here is why this subject should be interesting to you." Then the child experiences the magic of why. The reason for what he or she is doing becomes crystal clear. It's the first step toward motivation, because it gives young people a sense of purpose, and whenever you give people purpose, you give them drive.

GETTING RID OF THE BUSY WORK

A teacher needs to recognize that a young person's mind is built to wander and it's built to wonder. Wondering is really a beautiful thing in a child, and it is what we crush when we say, "Don't ask so many questions." But because the mind is also inevitably going to wander at that age, it is important to get rid of distractions. I call it the development of a laser mentality. A laser is light so focused that it can cut steel. Or think of a magnifying glass: It can focus light to a pinpoint that can start a fire. Focus creates a burning desire to succeed and cuts way down on wasted time and effort.

Students often feel frustrated with busy work that doesn't seem to lead to any result. On the first day that I meet my players, when they're freshmen, when they sit down in the classroom with me, I tell them that I am going to spend zero minutes doing two things: 1) lying to you, and 2) giving you busy work.

Some young people initially perceive what I give them to be busy work, so we talk about where that impression came from. It came from high-school classrooms where a teacher walked into the room and just asked the kids to get out their textbooks and independently rewrite a page or answer some end-of-chapter questions—and most importantly, "Be quiet while you're doing it!" That happens because the teacher isn't prepared, not because the student isn't prepared. And the kids get irritated. They feel their time is being wasted. And it is.

A lot of inner-city public schools function more as holding facilities than as schools, and that reality becomes how education is perceived. We must change that. That's why I emphasize that I don't believe in the concept of busy work. In fact, whenever the idea of busy work comes up in my classroom, I will sarcastically say, "Oh, you're right. I lie awake almost every night creating ways to watch you waste at least an hour a day…" They usually reply, "Point well taken, Coach." Everything we do will have a defined result. My students and I talk about the strength of asking questions, about never being afraid to ask why. After all, I tell them, if they knew the subject, they would be the teacher. They are there because they don't know, and so it is natural to have questions.

By creating an environment open to inquiry and challenge, a teacher or a coach is saying, "Look, don't do anything because I said so; do it because you know why, and if you don't know why, just ask."

BAXTERISM

Don't do anything because I said so; do it because you know why, and if you don't know why, just ask.

This is the foundation of a trusting and empowering classroom environment. The implication is this: "I'm not afraid of your wondering. I'm not afraid of your critical thinking or your questions." I believe in offering students the opportunity to question everything yet I challenge them to keep an open mind for the answer. In our classrooms we say "it's OK to not understand; but it's not OK to not understand and not ask a question." "I didn't understand" is not an acceptable explanation for low achievement, rather an excuse offered for why something didn't get done. People who don't have answers often are afraid of questions.

BAXTERISM

It's OK to not understand; but it's not OK to not understand and not ask a question.

HOW TO SHUT A YOUNG MIND DOWN

When you ask why, one of two things often happens: You get a clearer picture and understanding, or the instructor realizes there's a better way. Some of my greatest aha! moments as a teacher have come from realizing the student has a good point and a unique way of looking at things. "Wow!" I say to myself. "So that's how he sees it!" An instructor doesn't always have to have every answer on the spot. It's good sometimes to go home and think it over and admit that you need time to think about it. The kid who asked the question then feels validated and empowered. Seeing the teacher grappling with the answer propels the child to a new height of curiosity.

When you have been a career teacher, you become consistently aware of the patterns. In fact, as a football coach, whenever I clinic other coaches, I say my drills come from two places: 1) for skills that a player is going to have to repeatedly do, and 2) to avoid a problem that I know we will have. You see the same level of inexperience every time a new crop of students walks into your classroom. Your expertise can actually separate you from them unless you humble yourself to look at life from their perspective and what it must be like to be new to something. A favorite phrase of mine comes from Dr. Wayne Dyer's book *The Power of Intention,* "When you change the way you look at things, the things you look at change." I literally say it every day. There's no place for a sense of arrogance or dismissal in the classroom.

> ## BAXTERISM
> When you change the way you look at things, the things you look at change.

Instead of appealing to the magic of why, a teacher can easily shut the students down. Here's how to do it: When a student asks you why, just say, "I don't know," or "That's the way we've always done it." Or here's the king of the shutdowns: "Because I said so." When you say those things to students, they become less and less likely to think critically and creatively to solve a problem. If you instead appeal to their curiosity and innate desire to know why and help them build upon that, they will line up at your desk to find out how. They're going to come to your office after class: "Hey, tell me more about this. How do I find this out?"

I have found that my ability to have a breakthrough with my students depends a lot on how much teachers have burned them previously. Some have had good experiences. I do know there are many dedicated teachers out there and many others who mean well, but I am confident in my role in trying to overcome the problems that our educational system has presented. I want to do my part to instill, and reinforce, the love of learning.

What I have found is that many students have been laundered through the grades. They are in the mode of busy work, and that's how they see school. Some seem to have lost their curiosity about the world around them. In such cases, it takes me longer to build the vision that what I am teaching them is all about life skills, and solving problems, and thinking critically. It's not just assignments and homework, day after day. You have to build meaning into what they are doing, and as they gain experience they will come to value it.

THE BEST PAYDAY

I've gotten to the point in my life and my career where I'm actually trying to inspire new teachers as well as the students I see every day. Two things have come into great focus for me, and this is what I tell any young teachers who are my peers.

First, I tell them this: If you're going to do this long-term, as a profession, it's your job to plant, even though you might not see the seed growing. The harvest can take years. But almost all teachers with enough experience will tell you that their best payday was when a student came back to say how much they meant to that student. Those are the richest of paydays. You realize that you have been the person of influence that you set out to be.

The second thing that I tell young teachers is that they need to be a strong leader. A classroom is a pack, with group dynamics and a pecking order. If the teacher or coach isn't leading firmly, somebody else in that room will certainly take over the role, and the teacher will lose control. It's as Jack Welch says in his book *Control Your Destiny or Someone Else Will:* "you have to put yourself in charge."

That leads to respect, and it lasts a lifetime. Years later, when a former student thanks a teacher, that teacher knows it was all worthwhile. That teacher instilled in another human being the magic of why and the inspiration for future learning.

— CLINT'S FIELD NOTE —

When I showed up at Fresno State and joined the other players in listening to Coach Baxter's strategy sessions, I found myself saying, "Yes, Coach" over and over. He stopped me at one point and said, "Hey, cut it out with all that 'Yes, Coach' crap. If you understand what I'm saying, that's great, and if you don't, ask me about it. You don't need to keep saying yes, yes, yes." To which I replied, "Yes, Coach."

As he told us many times, "people buy into ideas, not

BAXTERISM

People buy into ideas, not orders.

There's no reason for failure when success is offered every day.

Manage your little voice.

orders". And if you don't understand why, then ask. "There's no reason for failure when success is offered every day". Early in our instruction, he taught us about "managing our little voice"—you know, the little voice in your head that spews negativity, and questions the validity of everything being said. "That's BS."

Before Coach Baxter introduced us to the wisdom of such statements, it was common practice for us, as students, if we didn't understand something or why we were doing it, to say, "This is stupid," or "This teacher is way off base," or "I'm not doing this." Instead of asking why or attempting to gain an understanding of purpose, we would just stop participating and thereby have a stand-off with the teacher.

But when someone comes along and tells you that if you don't understand the why of something, just ask and we will figure it out together, you start managing the little voice that used to limit you. If we thought something was stupid, we were required to ask about it and find out why and take ownership of our attitude. We simply weren't allowed to excuse anything as stupid and nonsensical without questioning why we felt that way. It's the ultimate in self-accountability.

I believe that when faced with a situation, you have three choices: You can accept it, change it, or leave it. There are those who accept Academic Gameplan and excel, because it's a given that they will have to go through it. That will not change. Others think they're too cool and fight it as extra work and an affront to their free time, only to find themselves struggling academically and truly losing their freedom. That's when they finally accept. They finally see why it was so important.

Coach Baxter helped me build my why. He took me from living someone else's expectations of me to living my own expectations. So when I said, "Yes, Coach," I was showing myself as the adopter of someone else's vision. I might as well have been saying, "Yes, Mom." I took orders better than most kids, and my transcript reflected it. But I had not taken ownership of my why. Coach Baxter wanted to make sure I had my own vision.

I know what he means when he talks about the "magic of why" and the "laser mentality." After all, he personally showed me. The energy of a stadium changes when a player goes out to kick a field goal. The focus turns to just one guy—whether he'll perform or choke—and a game, of course, can hinge on just those few points. I would find myself with 1.35 seconds to perform a task that could change the outcome of a game, while 50,000 or more people watched—and not all of them encouraging. You can imagine what went through my head.

Coach Baxter would send me to the field in such instances, with three parting words: "Pound your target!" His words inspired and motivated. He boiled down all the training into an expression of focus and attention. Kicking, like golf, is a highly technical endeavor. If you think too much about what you're doing, you can be paralyzed, as any golfer knows who has tried to perform while everyone around him offers different advice. One must avoid the internal head games. And Coach's three simple words took all that away.

Those words—"Pound your target!"—put me in a tunnel-like state where the only thing I saw was my result. The waving hands, the screaming fans, the flashing scoreboard, the crap-talking defensive players, they would all disappear from my consciousness as my energy focused, like a laser, on my target. Without saying it, he was telling me to trust my training, believe in my technique, and just let go. When I listened, it worked. If I didn't, I risked the consequences.

Coach Baxter is a master at simplifying complex concepts and tasks to make them digestible and easy to execute. This is where he separates himself as a teacher. In life, we will all face the booing crowds and various levels of adversity. We all risk choking if we let the distractions steal our focus. Coach Baxter believed in the idea of teaching targets, and that if I simply focused on "pounding my target" that concept would be central to my success. It worked on the field, and off, and it still does.

CHAPTER 7

The Power of

Grandpa Owen hit the brakes on the pickup truck and peered across the field and then looked at my cousin Matt and me, sitting next to him. "What will they think of next?"

"Grandpa, what are you talking about?" I asked.

"Right over there," he said, pointing to a machine in the field. "That's a nine-row corn planter."

Grandpa Owen, who was actually my cousin's grandfather, was about 90 years old at the time. He was born in 1902, and died when he was 98, at the turn of the new millennium. If his observation seems odd, consider that when he was a youngster, his family plowed with horses on their northern Indiana farm. In his century-long life, he saw 99 percent of the technological advances in the history of the planet.

When he was 92, he told Matt and me: "You know, the paper's going to do a story about me retiring. Hell, I'm not retiring. I'm just not going to farm all 350 acres." He paused and then said, "I want to show you boys something." He took us out to see a new combine that he had bought.

"Grandpa," I said, "I have to ask—those combines cost $200,000. Why are you financing a new combine when you're 92 years old?"

"Finance?" he said. "Hell, I paid cash." He'd lived through the great crash and other troubled times and he was saving money in his bedroom. After he passed away, there was a small fortune in refunds from the many years of pop bottles that he'd been piling up in the barn.

At the time he was born, farming had changed little in thousands of years. By the time he died, his combine had an air-conditioned cab, AM/FM stereo, and GPS. Such was the technological change during his life span. The law of the jungle in primitive society was survival of the fittest. In the information age, it has become survival of the most adaptable. My grandfather saw the advent of the automobile age, the space age, and the computer age. From his perspective, just the changes in farm equipment kept him busy enough. With every new technical development, he had to learn how to fix things differently. He had to adapt his technique.

One of the things I've learned as a football coach is it doesn't matter what you do on offense; it doesn't matter what you do on defense; it matters what you do when it breaks. Because if you can't fix it, whatever it is, it's dead. Once you have a big enough why, you naturally seek out the how, and that comes down to adapting your technique. What are the steps that it's going to take to get the job done?

We are at a period of time when we are witnessing the greatest technological advancements in the history of Earth, and yet we're doing the worst job ever of teaching technique, not to mention building a big-enough why. Without the why, the how is meaningless.

"HEY, LIBERACE!'

I was born on what I consider the cusp between a simpler time and technology—that is, by today's standards—and the wonders of the decades to come. My grandparents and parents grew up listening to radio and didn't have a TV. When I was small, our television was black and white. We took baths, not showers. When we dialed a phone call at my grandmother's house, we were on a party line, meaning we shared the line with several other homes and there was always the chance that somebody might be eavesdropping on the conversation. Times have changed immensely, and we in the later generations have had plenty of adapting to do, too.

I spent part of my boyhood on my grandparents' farm. My sister and I spent weekends and summers there, an hour away from our Chicago apartment with our mother.

I can't ever remember not playing sports. As soon as my eyes opened each day, I was outside running, jumping, chasing, or throwing something. I didn't know there was any other option. When my parents said, "Go out and play," I didn't know what else to play besides sports. We didn't grow up watching much TV because my mom would always tell us to shut off the idiot box and go do something productive. I still see the TV as the idiot box. I rarely even watch sports on TV. I'd rather be participating in the sport than watching others play it.

To me, going to school felt sort of like having a low-grade headache. I could function, but I wasn't exactly excited about it. Football was exciting. So was baseball, hockey, and basketball. We played them all. But academics didn't have anywhere near as much allure. I had trouble seeing the point of what I was studying. Nor could I get into the piano lessons that my mom decided my sister and I would take. She bought an old piano and all of a sudden it appeared in our home and along came a piano teacher one Wednesday afternoon. The piano lesson started at four o'clock. So did the whiffle ball game out front in the street.

I appreciate now that my mom was trying to make a well-rounded person out of me. That was her dream for my sister and me. But at the time, all I could think was there were five guys outside and they needed one more for three on three, and when would this lesson ever end? And after the lesson, I had to have dinner, another delay that my mom was putting in my way. Imagine, wanting your children to be well-nourished. I could almost hear the guys calling, "Hey, Liberace, let's get going!"

TRAFFIC JAM ON THE INFORMATION HIGHWAY

I hadn't reached the level of maturity to understand my mother's sacrifices and dreams for her children. That appreciation comes much later for virtually any kid. In fact, usually, we don't appreciate our parents until we become parents. We don't value things that we haven't experienced in life. But parents still must do what's right and instill those values. So must teachers, and coaches. They must continue to plant, and to adapt to changing times.

The changes in our technological society continue at a maddening pace. Ever more distractions pull children away, some far more tempting than the TV set. Young people text and tweet and download their apps and seem in a world apart at times. Technological change and the need to adapt are nothing new. When the farmer went from hoe to disk, that was a new application on the old concept of tilling the soil. It was an "app," if you will. But today's rapid change can lead to frustration and paralysis. The information age becomes the overwhelming age.

I just went to school every day doing what I was supposed to do but not knowing why I was doing it that way, not knowing what the point of the subject was. My mother was a single parent working every single day, and when she came home, she made dinner and did the laundry. She did it all herself. She was always concerned about how we were doing and always willing to help with any assignment or project but she was hardly looking over our shoulder and examining our homework. It was just expected that it would be done.

As I got older and the educational requirements became more technical, I began to execute less effectively to the point where my grades reflected it. My mom was not an uninvolved, uncommitted parent. She was anything but that. She would not compromise her goal of providing us a good education, no matter what it took, and the concept of going to college was non-negotiable. She managed somehow to send us to private schools on a single parent's meager income in 1977. She called the television "the idiot box," and would much prefer us to read or be active than to allow the energy leak that the TV seemed to provide. For me, it took years to bridge the generation gap and reach that level of appreciation. She figured out how to do it because she had an irrepressible why.

Today, technology defines the generation gap, not years. A generation gap is defined by how fast information and technology outdates itself. If you don't or cannot adapt, you're dead, you're irrelevant, you're out. Computers today seem obsolete the day after you buy them. When I tell somebody I have a three-year-old computer, they look at me as if I have a relic. A generation once was defined as about 20 years. Today, the gap can form in just a few years. There are students in college today studying a curriculum that will be outdated by the day they get their diploma, especially in information technology and the sciences. The fundamentals of learning do not change, and it is more imperative than ever that you are committed to being a lifelong learner and that you continually adapt.

Here's how I tell it to my players: "It's wonderful to be a student athlete. You're an athlete because it's fun. If it's not fun, don't play. And being an athlete will bring you benefits in your health and wellness, your fitness and nutrition. But still, at the end of the day, "you're going to be an athlete for part of your life but you're going to be a student for the rest of your life." In today's information jungle, if you are not committed to lifelong learning, you will be crushed because information is outdating itself every day. It is vitally important for your long-term competitiveness in business and industry that you develop a process of problem solving, studying and continuing education."

BAXTERISM

You're going to be an athlete for part of your life but you're going to be a student for the rest of your life.

The Internet has changed everything forever. People feel an insatiable urge for access all the time. In 2009 they built a new library at Fresno State for $105 million dollars. One day, the college president Dr. John Welty and I were flying to a game together, and I asked him, "Why did we spend $105 million on a library when everybody just uses Google?" The concept of a library can now seem archaic. Once, we thumbed through card catalogs. Then it was a big deal when you could look up books on CD-Rom. That's all outdated. Today, you can run keyword searches on old books and newspapers, and much more.

We indeed have easier access to information, and that's all the more reason we must adapt, or lose out. That's why it is so important that kids learn to problem solve. In today's culture of helicopter parents, so many kids are driven from organized activity to activity and don't go out for free play. But that's where they would learn to solve problems. That's where they learn the how. Those boys playing whiffle ball outside my window had to adapt without me. Otherwise, the game just wouldn't go on.

Today adults orchestrate everything. Parents hover, and they start wanting to win the game more than the kids do. They even come to believe—and I have seen this in recruiting—that their son specializes in football, and not only that, but in a particular position. That's insanity to me. If a high-school kid wants to play any and all sports, he should do so because most won't play beyond that level and the variety makes them more rounded athletically. And yet the trend in our technology-aided world continues to be specializing, earlier and earlier, and I don't think that's good for the development of the whole person.

ACADEMIC GAMEPLAN, LLC: LAPTOP LUNACY CONTINUES

When my daughter Kelly turned 12 in 2009, I said to my wife, "I don't remember being that old when I was 12." I explained that Kelly seemed far ahead of where I was at that age, with resources and opportunities and access that I probably didn't have until I was twice her age. That's how much things have changed in just one traditional generation. Technology has changed so much, and education is being driven today by technology. My mom, who was born in 1939, went to a one-room school in Westville, Indiana, in the 1940s. In 2013 my daughters Kelly and Mckenzie are taking online summer courses in economics and government. That's the vast difference that I see when I look just one generation back and one generation ahead.

Information used to trickle, like water out of a clogged faucet. When I went to school in the 1960s and 1970s, it flowed more freely, fast enough to quench my thirst, anyway. Today information is coming at us and it's out of an open fire hydrant. Information comes at us so fast that it is often intimidating. If you do not learn, at least fundamentally, how to process, organize, incorporate, prioritize, and use that information, you cannot survive in the modern age.

Our students are immersed in a world of Technology-Developed **ADD** (TDADD) and suffer from the **F**ear-**O**f-**M**issing-**O**ut syndrome (FOMO), and we are doing the worst job ever of teaching the technique and discretion required to be productive and not distracted by this technology.

Several years ago, when my kids were in middle school, they entered what the school called a "laptop program." At parents night, I asked why they felt laptops were so critical. "Well," our host said, "if you don't have a laptop, you're not going to be able to compete with the way education is going." I pointed out that education doesn't come from a laptop. Learning how to use one is useful, like learning to type, but it isn't a solution in itself. In fact, it just opens the fire hydrant. It douses kids with an information torrent that they may not be able to handle.

As parents, you may not realize that when you succumb to your child's "need" for his or her own smart phone or laptop, you are, in fact, handing that child a full flowing fire hydrant with no adjust wrench. With a smart phone you are actually handing your child more technology than was in the Apollo 11 space ship that we sent to the moon in 1969. PG 13 is an appropriate initialism because this is about the age when parents hand their children *"the source of constant distraction."* We freely hand them the technology without regard for the technique of how to use it and the discretion required to not be distracted by it, but be productive with it. A parents biggest worry seems to be "what if they lose it." PG 2013: That's the parental guidance required in 2013 and beyond…

See if you recognize anyone you know in this story…

We went to a wedding recently, and before we went into the reception, I asked my kids to leave their cell phones in the car. They looked at me as if I were some kind of outer-space alien! In keeping with how I have raised them, of course they asked, "Why?" Let's just say that I was armed and dangerous for this conversation…

I said, "We are going to see a lot of people we haven't seen in a long time—and you will probably meet some new and interesting people." After all, this was Bear Pascoe's wedding. He is a former player of mine and a tight end for the New York Giants. "I don't want to see you sitting at the table in your own little virtual cell-phone world, texting and Facebooking when the only Facebook that's important are the real faces sitting next to you!" What I've found through my players and my own children is that anytime an interpersonal environment becomes new or even slightly uncomfortable, they withdraw into their own little "iWorld."

You have heard me say it throughout the book that "life is a team sport," which means your success will be defined by the network you can create. People who have learned to master creating and maintaining strong interpersonal relationships are people who will ultimately succeed. "You show

BAXTERISM

You show me your friends, and I'll show you your future.

me your friends, and I'll show you your future" is a mantra that I preach regularly to my players.

Within a short time, my daughters were asking for my car keys because they "needed" their phones. They were like junkies looking for a fix. Of course, I refused, and the rest of the evening was wonderful and we all enjoyed each other's company. FOMO is a real condition that we have created, and without intentional training, all of us are susceptible.

In our staff meeting room was a sign that read, "What you see is a result of what you are either coaching or allowing to happen, but one of the two is true." When you can accept this statement as fact, it will change the way you see teaching, parenting, and coaching.

On the drive home from the wedding, the satisfaction came when both girls admitted, "Wow, Dad, that was really fun, and I see why we left our phones in the car. We didn't realize how much we used our phones to escape certain situations while we check our text messages."

In 1990 Steven Covey wrote a book called *The 7 Habits of Highly Effective People,* a bestseller that emphasizes "restoring the character ethic" in all our dealings. There are fundamentals that are timeless foundations for excellence in business and personal relationships. Just as a house must be built on a strong foundation, we can build effective lives if we put those rules, fundamentals, and techniques in place so that all we do rises on top of them.

The how that we develop and bring forward in Academic Gameplan deals with the processing, internalizing, and strategic planning for all of the information that's coming at the student through the fire hydrant. Somebody has to help that young person— maybe more than ever in the history of education—understand the techniques to learn more effectively. Students are falling through the cracks, not necessarily because they lack interest but more likely because they are trying to deal with so very much coming at them.

TALENT IS THE RAW MATERIAL; TECHNIQUE IS THE FINISHED PRODUCT

I often hear about how much talent we have at USC. I have been quick to point out a basic truth that I have observed: "Talent is the raw material, technique is the finished product." Your level of talent is secondary to your level of execution, and execution comes from developing your technique.

Most college football recruiters are dealing with the very top talent in the nation. Even among those athletes who matriculate to play college football—the best of the best—there will always be different levels of talent. At the end of the

> # BAXTERISM
>
> Talent is the raw material, technique is the finished product.

day, talent is relative, as is intelligence. All of us possess different gifts. What will make the difference for each of us is the ability to access what gives us the competitive edge, and as Jack Welch observed, if you don't have a competitive advantage, then don't compete. I would add to that: Don't compete if you can't create a competitive advantage. That's what coaches do. They develop talent and create advantages. They help a young person discover that how.

The issue that we're talking about is technique. At any level of learning, technique is critical to success and advancement, and yet it is not being addressed in the classroom, where the teachers focus on their subject, not on skills. Again, this is why the paradigm shift would come from the edge, where you wouldn't expect it. Coaches go out on the field every day and know intuitively that if they don't teach fundamentals, the players will have no ability to execute the scheme. If the players can't function individually, they can't hang together as a team. Yet in the classroom we have teachers who go in the first day and fire up the assembly line and just start teaching their subject without regard for skills and techniques needed to support it.

Drill sergeants also know what it takes to make men function at the level at which they will need to perform when they're under the gun, so to speak. We send soldiers to basic training to learn the techniques and fundamentals that will serve them well in battle.

Let me share a poem by Bob Bennett, the longtime baseball coach at Fresno State.

THE I'S IN TEAM

There are no I's in teamwork
It has often been said.
Examine the statement.
Don't be misled.

Each player has two eyes.
Each pair of eyes is important to the team.
These eyes see the little details
That execute the scheme.

Teamwork is not just a word.
In the spelling of the word there are no I's,
But to carry teamwork out, there are many
Of these, there is no surprise.

I count is important to remember.
Another is I care.

Don't forget that I am responsible.
A tenet of teamwork is "I will share."

I will endure.
I will prevail.
I will compete.
Any hurdle I will assail.

Integrity I will supply.
Honor I will uphold.
I will be trustworthy.
Truth I will extol.

Tasks I will finish.
Excellence I will pursue.
I will be dependable
And see each battle through.

Spell the word correctly
But remember, the I's make teamwork live.
So don't forget the I's
For they have so much to give.

I will provide leadership.
I have compassion that each team needs.
I am committed provides the fiber.
Without the I's no team succeeds.

Copyright Bob Bennett 2002
Poem reprinted with permission of Bob Bennett.

People often say that there is no "I" in *team*, and it's true that the teamwork is all-important. But in another sense there are a lot of

I's. Each individual has to function at a high level in his or her role within the team.

THE NEED FOR A FILTER

It's more important than ever that we recognize that young people are having a difficult time compartmentalizing and prioritizing. The much-ballyhooed technology that has become a part of every classroom is actually detracting from their ability to focus.

As a parent myself, as well as a college football coach, I have some personal perspective here. We have two girls in high school as I write this, and I've sought to eliminate their distractions. Kelly and Mckenzie are bright young people, so if we were to see any slip in their grades, I would know it's not a matter of ability. The problem is in the management of distractions. Those distractions have come via 500 television channels, the Internet, Facebook, Twitter, Instagram, texting, video chatting, Youtube, and more.

Jill and I had to make a rule in our house that the cell phones get turned off at 9 p.m., no questions asked. The computer is to be used at the dining room table and it never goes up to a bedroom. The computer in and of itself isn't evil. The cell phone in and of itself isn't evil. None of this technology is evil. But the application of it is very, very damaging if not managed and if discretion is not taught. We have seen what computers can do for us. Those apps, some of them, hold the potential to make our lives better, just as the farmer with the hoe welcomed the invention of the disk. But because these devices stream such tremendous volumes of information, they also stream tremendous volumes of distractions.

The cell phone provider is not Sprint or AT&T but rather the adult that purchases the phone and pays the bill. It is clearly the job of the provider to establish the ground rules and teach the discretion necessary to allow the child to succeed. We have made it emphatically clear in our house that the phone "is a tool and not a toy." Being productive with the tool requires technique and we have taught the technique every step of the way.

In our house the rule is; the phone gets turned off and I mean completely powered off when homework starts and stays that way until it's done or there is a distinct break in the process. Why? It's that way for the same reason that an airplane pilot will ask that "all electronic devices get powered off before take off." When asked why, they will explain that "they do not want to risk any interference with the aircrafts navigational system." Interesting! Our policy is based on the same line of thinking. Keep in mind that it often takes longer to recover from an interruption than the interruption took itself.

Doing homework or work of any kind for that matter is a navigational framework of going from "chaos to concept and process to product" An occasional interruption is manageable but constant interruption will definitely cripple the process. Today, one simple cell phone can stream enough distraction to bring even the most basic creative process or work flow to its knees. It is a gateway to an information super highway that can and will be used against you in the court of creativity. It is technological water boarding on steroids.

Imagine the teenage distractions that come via the phone that streams non-stop sounds that chime, ring, ding and dong. These sounds alert them to vitally important notifications of incoming text messages, instagram, twitter, facebook, snapchats, google alerts, emails, likes, comments, calendar reminders, friend requests, followers, favorites, retweets and phone calls if those even exist any more.

I feel like installing a speaker system in my house and via the intercom make a nightly announcement: Good evening young ladies and welcome aboard flight 168 to success. From the flight deck this is your captain John speaking. In a few moments we'll be checking your homework for accuracy and completeness. For your convenience you'll find a safety briefing card with the house rules on the refrigerator door in case you forgot them since last night. We require that you give us your careful attention. The use of all electronic devices is prohibited at all times as they can interfere with the homework navigational system. All portable electronic devices such as iPods and cell phones must be turned off and remain off for the duration of our flight. In the event one of you little FOMOs feels light-headed due to lack of contact with the outside world, oxygen masks will drop down in front of you. Please pull the mask down toward your face and place the mask over your nose and mouth. If you are studying next to someone acting like a child, please attend to yourself first, then the child. Breathe normally; the feeling will pass. Thank you for your attention. Now sit up, lean forward, act interested and attack your homework.

Today, if someone in a person's social network decides that he or she is bored and wants to send a text rather than do homework, their friends' phones start beeping. Smart phones go off twenty-four hours a day. I noticed that whenever my daughters' phones made those noises, they would stop what they were doing, wherever they were, and immediately look at the phone. You have probably seen what I have witnessed at a restaurant: four people at a table, and all of them staring at their phones rather than chatting with one another.

My kids do get As, and I'm proud of them. But as a dad, I wanted to help them manage those distractions so that they could think straight. I didn't want them to resent me or think me old-fashioned, but I was resolved to do something about the situation. Though the devices aren't evil, the values that the media can stream to you are potentially very evil and damaging. Keep in mind that young people in their teenage years do not and cannot have the life experience to interpret everything they say.

I'm astounded, for example, that many parents seem oblivious to the fact that pornography can so easily find its way into their children's lives, even when those children don't go actively looking for it. Sexual predators wait to pounce online, and some prey on very young children. These are hardly free spirits, though it takes wisdom to recognize that.

We're all familiar with the statement, "Parental discretion is advised." I often feel there's little substance behind that statement— almost as if it's used as a marketing ploy to entice attention—and I think parents don't act on that call to action. It means parents should have the life experience and perspective to help young people interpret what they are watching and should be involved.

Today's parents may feel frustrated at their children's incessant social networking, but every generation of adults has had a difficult time with something that the next generation of kids was doing: their styles, their music, their slang. Every generation also thinks the younger one is ungrateful. But that attitude of gratitude comes from only one thing, and that's life experience. It gives us perspective. In time, we all learn to be thankful.

I wanted my children to see that there are other ways to do things, and the house rules were meant to help them filter out the distractions. So we restricted those cell phones, and we got rid of Instagram. We got rid of Twitter. When I told my daughter Kelly that Facebook was out of the picture too, she protested.

"You don't understand!" she told me. "My coach uses Facebook to tell all of us when the practices will be, and the teachers use it to send us our assignments."

She was pointing out to me a legitimate use of the social media. When it's used as a tool, all is well; when it's used as a toy, we have better things to do. It's an attempt to reach out and communicate useful skills and necessary information. It's not that adults should teach young people to shun the social media. Rather, they should teach them to use these devices and applications wisely in the spirit of forming healthy connections.

These are tools, not toys, and parental discretion is advised.

We were with our team recently at the Sun Bowl banquet, which is a big community function before the game. Both teams and both coaching staffs and prominent people from the community come to those banquets. At each table, a player from each team sits with six members of the community. We looked out over the room and we were horrified. We saw players from USC and Georgia Tech, two major universities, sitting at tables with six strangers—all good, hard-working members of the community who had paid for the honor of being there—and the players were staring into their phones. Instead of interacting, they were putting up a wall. They seemed to have no idea how to introduce themselves or carry on a simple conversation with a stranger.

After that, I made it a key part of Academic Gameplan to make sure that young people know the *real* meaning of social networking. The cell phone and laptop actually can become shields from the rest of society. What I see is a tendency in young people to pull out their cell phones whenever they feel uncomfortable or aren't sure what to do or how to act. They can retreat into their own customized little world, all the while displaying body language that says, "I'm too busy to talk. I have something more important than you here." When I was that age, the "idiot box" that my mom wanted us to get away from was the television. Today, the idiot box fits in your hand.

If parents see a slip in a student's grades, they need to get to the source of the distraction and not just treat the symptom. A lot of things can sidetrack a student, including emotional and social issues, but a major one is the distraction of a cell phone or the Internet. It is critically important that we work to identify the source and to filter out the distractions. People are born to grow, to develop, to learn, to compete, and we must not let anything interfere with that.

LEARNING AT A SANE PACE

Today's classrooms are far different from the ones many of us remember. If you walk into a classroom today, you might see the same teacher you had in years past, but now he or she is presenting lessons via PowerPoint, projected from a laptop, or streamed from the Internet. Students pull a phone, laptop, or tablet (not the paper kind) out of their backpack and use them to take notes, among other things. They can even make an audio recording of the lecture and listen to it later. When the teacher writes the homework assignment on the board, the students don't take the time to write it down. They just use their phone to take a picture of the board and text it to themselves, or to one of their friends who's not in class. What has changed in education isn't the subjects so much as how they are delivered. Today technology drives education.

There's something to be said for slowing down. When the teacher used to write the highlights on the blackboard in chalk, and you had to copy them down, your brain had a chance to think, to process, to store the lesson away for later use. When you take a snapshot with your phone's camera, you lose something that every good teacher knows is important, and that's the value of repetition and pausing to reflect. As my colleague Coach Steve Hagen would say, "He who does the work, does the learning." A camera shot doesn't allow for that. It's like taking a yellow highlighter and marking every sentence on every page. Have you really filtered anything? Have you internalized what's important?

Students need to read—and at their own pace. Often they are frustrated because they feel that they must just be slow readers. But when you're reading something you're unfamiliar with, you shouldn't be a fast reader. You should take it at a pace that lets you process it. Parents should let their children slow down and focus instead of jamming their schedules and brains and then wondering, "What's wrong with my kid?" Why isn't he competitive? Why doesn't she like school? Why is he underperforming?" They may get one diagnosis or another about a learning disability, but when I was in school we didn't call it ADD; we called it daydreaming.

When a kid has trouble focusing, he needs to learn technique, and that's what I teach. Every coach intuitively knows that when a player struggles with a skill, the first thing you do is slow it down and isolate the difficulty, breaking a fast-paced activity into its segments.

BAXTERISM

Slow and right is better than fast and wrong.

Once the player has learned to deal with the individual parts, he can assemble them into the whole and do it fast. Slow and right is better than fast and wrong.

Technology also has introduced the concept of distance learning and online courses into education. Technology actually has worked to destroy the fabric of interpersonal relationships. Businesses are built on relationships, because all products and services are purchased by people. The relationship between Clint and me has evolved from coach and player to colleagues on a mission to co-create change for students. Relationships add a depth and richness to our lives. We need one another.

And yet you can get a full degree online, streamed to your home. As I mentioned, my daughter is taking an online summer course in government and economics. "Why not take it as a summer class?" I asked her. "Dad, that would mean I'd have to sit in a classroom for eight weeks." In Academic Gameplan, I ask students the rhetorical question, "Are you in school for an education or a degree?" And the question always generates a lot of discussion. Online education is another example of delivering the subject without the skill. We lose touch with the whole person.

I see every class as an opportunity to teach reading, writing, and problem solving, and as an opportunity for young people to work through problems and issues with a mentor. As I say often, "life is a team sport" and the learning process should reflect this.

HARNESSING THE POWER OF HOW

The magic of why, which we talked about earlier, is the hub of everything we're doing. It is the center of the wagon wheel, and all the other elements are the spokes. The best teachers, the best parents, the best coaches, and the best businesses all build a big-enough why.

To be digested, information must be separated into catego-

> **BAXTERISM**
>
> To solve a problem, you go from chaos to concept. Then process to product.

ries. To solve a problem, you go from chaos to concept. Then process to product. Students do that when they work through the steps to produce a ten-page paper. They do it when they organize a study guide. They do it when they break down a 350-page reading assignment into daily chunks that they can execute before a deadline. They learn a process that produces a product. Keep in mind, for all of this to work, everything in education, business, and life rests on the idea that "the deadline triggers the process."

BAXTERISM

The deadline triggers the process.

In Academic Gameplan,[*] we offer a copyrighted system through which player and coach, or student and mentor, can interact. Parents can sit down with their children, review the Student GPS system, and ask what they did that day, or what they will do tomorrow, and later. They begin to build a task list together, and as they do so, not only do the details of the day come together, but others surface. In the process of writing down and building a prioritized daily task list, the speed bumps and roadblocks become apparent. For example, the student reveals he's upset about something and why. Perhaps it's something some other kid is doing, or he doesn't understand a teacher or finds the teacher unapproachable. The two of them begin to discuss how to handle these situations, and it is from such discussions that relationships grow.

We've offered Academic Gameplan since 1999, but in the last several years parents have been coming to me and saying, "Coach, you know what you really need? You need an app." Imagine. Maybe I could make some money putting such a thing out there in this app-frenzied environment, but that would make me part of the problem.

See page 175 for a special offer.

I'm not saying that apps are a problem or ineffective, but I do believe that the fundamentals and a template for thinking need to be accomplished before we rely completely on the app world. Our paper planner accomplishes a great deal in building a fundamental base for strategic planning, and a template for thinking and problem-solving. I don't want anyone to be hostage to the belief that a smart phone has real power. Batteries run out, and the phone is struck dumb. Motherboards sizzle. Hard drives come upon hard times. I'm looking to build the intelligence that puts the "smart" in smart phone.

Never mind the technology for now. We need to teach young people the process of strategic planning. They need to learn how to build that daily list and keep score for themselves to make sure their numbers add up to their goals. Once they have mastered the fundamentals of how to go from chaos to concept, from process to product, they may be ready for an app if they can use it with wisdom. An app does not solve a problem. The user solves the problem. "Garbage in, garbage out," after all, is a mantra of computer science. It reflects a much older expression: "As you sow, so shall you reap."

"Life is a team sport." Though it's important to do your independent work and stand out as an individual, life is all about the relationships that you create in your family, in school, in business, and in the community. We're on the road together, helping one another find the way.

When I talk in public, I often ask people what they would do if they had an extra hour to spend each day. Five years ago they often said they would do more reading. Today they often say they would take a break, go for a nature walk, get some exercise. So why don't they read more? Why don't they go for those walks? Books don't beep, and nature doesn't ring. They don't demand your attention the way our gadgets do, the ones that suck away so much of our time. We must establish our priorities and pursue them. We must manage the distractions. We must harness the power of how.

— CLINT'S FIELD NOTE —

Any athlete knows how fickle fans can be. I've heard it. One missed kick, and they all make comments. Those words are far more indicative of the type of person the fan is rather than the type of person the player is. One moment you can be a star, and the next you're a bum. Based on the outcome, I was considered a hero or zero. You're esteemed as a person of stature and strength if your foot connects with a ball and sends it between two sticks. In truth, ten other guys needed to do their job so that I could do mine. If they didn't, or if I made a mistake—and we're human—it became extremely easy to lose self-confidence. They love you or they hate you, and becoming obsessed with the outcome is only natural.

In other words, fans often judge us on the outcome, and that outcome, particularly for a kicker, is black and white. Never mind your dedication, work ethic, leadership, or community involvement. It only matters whether the ball goes through the uprights or not. That's how you're valued.

What Coach Baxter did for me, as a player, student, and a person, was to refocus that energy away from the outcome. He would say, "Clint, all that stuff is just a big energy leak. Don't ever let a negative influence live in your mind rent free. It's so easy to obsess about what might happen if you miss. That's

BAXTERISM

There's so much more to a person than his transcripts.

why he says, "I don't care about your grades. I don't care about your subjects. I only care about your process!" As he says, "There's so much more to a person than his transcripts." He wanted me to be concerned with how I spent a week preparing for a test rather than worry about whether I'll get an A or not. He wanted me to care more about the quality of focused practice reps than about whether the ball ended up through the uprights. He relieved me from the angst of obsessing over outcomes, the feeling that "Oh my God, I'd better make this kick, or get an A on this test, or my life is doomed to fall apart." So many kids feel that pressure. I did, and when I focused on my process, the pressure dissipated.

Coach Baxter has his players write personal constitutions, based on the question, "Who are you, and what do you represent?" I wrote one as a kicker. As a young player with a strong leg, I had a tendency to overkick. Young players often try hitting the ball too hard, and they lose accuracy. In my constitution, I wrote that I was on the field to put the team in a good position to win, and the only way I could do that would be "to take selfless passes at the ball," meaning that I was not going to be selfish and try to prove myself to the world, but rather, I was going to go out and do what was right for the team. My constitution consisted of several statements, all based on being a team player who trusts in his training and his coaching.

People have often asked me: "What are you thinking when the game is on the line and everyone is depending on you?" I have learned to focus. I go through my pre-kick process, I perform my checklists, take a deep breath, and then just let it happen."

Though it has been years since we were together at Fresno State, it seems as if Coach Baxter is often still coaching me when we chat. The relationship between coach and player never ends.

About the time that Coach Baxter was setting down his household rules for texting and using cell phones and other gadgets, he called me to talk about it. These devices are tools, he said, and nothing more. They can be useful for interaction, he said, but a lot of times they prevent that interaction in any meaningful way, and we really need to make sure our children understand that. These tools shouldn't be occupying their every moment, because that means the device is taking control of their lives. Today's students might feel empowered by all these new devices and tools, but really they are making the same old mistakes through a different medium. They photograph the notes on the board, or they record and e-mail an entire lesson, and then they don't know what to make of it. They lack a sensible process. They don't know how to use the tool.

His words hit home. Like him, I have two daughters, though mine are much younger. And I found myself immediately applying his advice in my own life. I'd often been waking up at four in the morning and responding to the beep of an e-mail, because I had the notion that e-mails demanded prompt attention. Often, they are just distractions. Because of the coaching role he still plays in my life, I know that in the years to come I will be protecting my own daughters from the distractions and dangers of the Internet.

As a student and athlete, I experienced how Coach established the team culture. We all lived by a set of rules and expectations. "One day," he would tell us, "when you are starting a family or starting a business, these will be your guiding principles. You will know how to do it." He often told us, "I don't care about your grades. I don't care about what courses you're in. I care about your process." He was helping us to be a successful person, not just a football player. He saw the husband, father, coworker we would eventually be.

On many teams, the players are just told what to do and they're expected to buy into it. I bought in because Coach made it clear that it would make a big difference in my life for the long haul. Few coaches insist that their players understand that what they are learning will help them immensely when they are building their own families or businesses. Few coaches help their players make the connection that what they're doing will make them a better person and able to create a better life for others as well.

I've learned so much about life from Coach Baxter, and I'm happy to spread the word. I was blessed to have been involved with five different NFL organizations, and no one at any of those stops had the impact or ability to relate to me the way Coach Baxter has. When you teach people about important fundamentals, they pass that on to others they care about, and it grows and it grows and it grows.

CHAPTER 8

Building the
FUNDAMENTALS

"Keep your eye on the ball," the T-ball coach tells five-year-old Jimmy, who is seriously contemplating that ball, perched on a tee over home plate. Jimmy swings, the ball plops, everyone cheers. It's a reasonable compromise for a tyke who just might have a few difficulties hitting a curve ball traveling at 80 miles an hour. For children at that age, the best introduction to baseball is a game that helps them work on their swing. Start with the fundamentals.

In spring training, major league players do the same thing. There you can see highly paid coaches over in the outfield working with highly paid players swinging at a ball on a tee. Essentially, they go back to the fundamentals when they are working out their swing.

At the highest level of competition, even the best hitters develop hitches or hiccups in their swing. If you're ever going to work out a swing problem, you have to slow down the process. Whether you are a 35-year-old major league baseball player or a five-year-old on a ball diamond for the first time, the fundamentals of how you develop a strong, powerful swing are taught the same way, using a tee.

A little kid playing T-ball is learning a lot more than just how to handle the bat. Parents encourage young people to play baseball and other sports so that they can experience being part of a team, working cooperatively with a group toward a common goal while developing individual strengths. Just as they're learning the basics of the swing, they're also learning how to get into the swing of life. They're learning life skills about getting along with people, problem solving, and competing for something they want, and those will be the building blocks for many other arenas in life.

Just what are the fundamentals? When you ask that question, people struggle for a definition. That's because the fundamentals differ depending on what you are talking about. Within every sport there is a set of basics for each position. It's likewise with life. The best coaches demand an emphasis on those building blocks so that the players can compete when the pressure is on. In any endeavor, reliance on and mastery of the fundamentals is the basis of what becomes competitive greatness.

IN THE SPIRIT OF THE GREEK TRIAD

The ancient Greeks believed that the development of the mind, the will, and the body were linked, and that one must be instructed in that triad for a well-balanced education. Athletics is essential to that balance.

In a highly technical sport such as football, more than half the preparation happens in the classroom. To play the game well—to play any game well—you need to be a thinker and cultivate the mind. You need a strong will to overcome the discouragement and adversity that comes with the learning process. We call it mental toughness, and we define it as "the ability to carry out a worthwhile decision after the emotion of making it has past." And of course, you need a strong, steady, and agile body. To be a well-rounded and truly educated person, one must develop in all three realms of that triad—and this viewpoint informs my objections to policies such as No Child Left Behind and high-stakes testing that limit curriculum and our children's range of experiences.

Invariably, when you see a list of the most highly respected coaches of all time, John Wooden's name would be high on the list. In his book *They Call Me Coach,* he outlines his "pyramid of success" and advises that "the difference between champions and near champions is the execution of tiny details." Great coaches, he points out, are great teachers. They get their point across, slow down the process, and get people to execute. To that I would add this observation: Great teachers are really great coaches. Coaching is the highest level of instruction.

Successful people surround themselves with coaches. Business people, for example, have an accounting team, legal representation, and other advisors. Many people seek counsel from priests and ministers, rabbis, and imams, and other religious coaches. We should surround ourselves with people who can take us where we're unable to take ourselves, who will hold us accountable, and who will help us bring balance and success to our lives.

Young people need to learn to set standards for themselves, based on the counsel of wise people, and it is likely that they will find those people in places other than their circle of friends. One of the things that I say to my players repeatedly, from the time I recruit them, is: "You show me your friends and I'll show you your future." People are meant to exist in groups, and in doing so, they do what the group does. When I see someone's circle of friends, I know that person is doing the things that the people in that circle are doing. People don't make themselves part of the group so that they can do things outside what the group is doing. Growth has much to do with the quality of the soil. Good growth does not occur in toxic soil.

Teaching and coaching are different instructional models. When I talk about the difference between teaching and coaching I am not talking classroom teacher versus athletic coach but, rather, the difference in the process. Teaching is an assembly line process. A teacher must progress through subject matter with only slight pauses because the bottom line is that there is only so much time to cover a body of material before the deadline. The state says, in essence, "You have to start here and you have to end here, because this is what's going to be on the standardized test." Therefore, the teacher's perspective must be, "I can slow down occasionally and answer some brief questions, but we must keep moving, ready or not." By comparison, coaching is a model based on mastery. We must take the time it takes, and find a process that will deliver results. There are no excuses; performance is the bottom line. The coach's perspective, however, is that "we're going to do this until either you get it or we run out of time." "And by the way you have to get it; failure is not an option. Coaching to me is the highest level of instruction, and the best classroom teachers actually coach their subject.

When students run into concepts they don't understand, the teacher keeps on going unless a student says, "Whoa, I need some help here." Even if the assembly line slows down for a bit, it soon speeds up again. Time pressure doesn't facilitate learning and you can forget mastery. *I am not criticizing teachers; rather, as a teacher myself, I am empathizing with them and the ridiculous standard to which they're asked to adhere.* What they often are asked to do is not in keeping with the spirit of the Greek triad.

FIRST THINGS FIRST

In coaching football, there are two levels of instruction. First come the fundamentals of how to block, how to tackle, how to run a route, how to catch and throw a pass and take a handoff. Then there's schematic instruction, which is the certain block you have to execute, the certain route you have to run, the certain defense you have to play.

The team's execution of the play has no chance of success without a firm grasp of the fundamentals. The schematics of football are built on top of rules, fundamentals, and techniques. Until those are in place, an athlete is likely to struggle to advance in the execution of the schematics. Likewise, until the basics are in place, a student is likely to struggle to advance in any subject, and yet those basics do not have a curriculum slot in schools.

Students need to be taught those basics, such as learning to take notes on a lecture. Students often try to rationalize that they're just not good note takers, and I tell them that nobody's a good note taker. After all, no one can write at a pace anywhere near as fast as someone else can talk. In Academic Gameplan I prove that, based on conversational speech, at best only a maximum of 10 percent of the actual spoken words can be captured on a page of notes. Note taking is hard to teach. In fact it's perhaps the toughest of all academic skills to teach. So much depends on how familiar the student is with the material. If Clint and I were both to sit through a lecture on finance and take notes, his would be far different from mine since he, with his finance degree, is on a higher level of understanding. I would be taking notes on terms and concepts that would be clear to him and therefore he may not even record.

Note taking is a fundamental, but even among the fundamentals each student must tailor the approach to his or her interest and level of experience. If your notes aren't the same as your classmates' notes, it just means you are at a different level or learn differently. And when it comes down to it, we are all slow note takers. Everyone feels alone in this, and yet we are all the same in this. We're all slower than we think we should be when we are dealing with unfamiliar material, but that doesn't mean we can't take notes well.

That holds true as well for reading effectively, and I say "effectively," not "rapidly." I also hear kids tell me all the time that they hate reading, or they're just too slow at it. Clint told me he was a slow reader. Yet he graduated with a 4.0 GPA in finance. A teacher may label a high-school kid by saying, "He is reading at a fourth-grade level." Why not consider that exciting? After all, the underlying message is that he can read. He just doesn't. The operative words are "is reading."

BAXTERISM

People who don't read have no distinct advantage over people who can't read.

"Coach, why do I have to read this book?" I sometimes hear. What I tell such students who "hate" reading is this: "People who don't read have no distinct advantage over people who can't read." The bottom line is if you want to read well or at a higher level, you simply have to read. Period. Little Johnny can read. He just chooses not to!

Though each of us is different, reading and note taking are among those academic skills that we need in order to execute. They are building blocks to success. Schools need to emphasize their importance, but they fail to do so.

WHY PEOPLE REMEMBER THEIR COACHES

When people recall the influential people in their lives, often it is a coach that makes the list. They tend to remember coaches more than teachers because the coach had a personal investment in their success and simply spent more time with them.

Many people can function as coaches in the lives of students, and not just in sports. The coach could be a music or drama instructor, or the editor of the student newspaper, or even the geometry teacher. What they have in common is that they see young people as more than just sponges sitting at desks. They get to know the person and his or her needs. A true coach will say, "Hey, why don't you stay half an hour and let's work on your swing," or "I think I see how you could deliver that line for the school play in a more powerful way. Let's take some time to work on it."

Coaches show investment and caring, and as a result become highly influential in young people's lives. Young people all deserve a coach who believes in them. It's an essential aspect of the coaching relationship: We will do this together, go through some trials and tribulations, and, together, we will figure it out. I have told everyone I've coached that we will hit some speed bumps, but we must trust in the process. We must have patience that we will accomplish our goals once we conquer these little challenges.

It's a serious responsibility, and all those in the role of coach, whether sports coach, parent, or teacher, must take a close look at how they interact with young people. These are not just trivial relationships. They play a central role in development. That's why it's important for parents and anyone else to exercise self-control at youth sporting events. Shouts of anger and impatience damage the coaching relationship.

"Anger is the enemy of instruction." When anger enters the equation, students have to process their own feelings first. Thus, any shot at gleaning the information exchanged has been lost. The kid ends up embarrassed and doesn't listen to the lesson. This is not building on fundamentals; it's more like tearing them down.

THE SEVEN SUCCESS Ts

Although I did have some good teachers, I've always hoped to make myself the teacher that I wish I'd had. I was a frustrated learner. To that end, I've focused my coaching on a process that we call the Seven Success Ts. Together, they make up a process necessary for success in any sport, subject, or discipline.

The seven Ts are attitude, terminology, training, tools, technique, time, and teamwork. You could think of this process as the thick extension cord that powers the hundreds of twinkling lights on a Christmas tree. They are in essence the fundamentals that I teach. Let's take a look at each.

Attitude

Attitude is the primary building block upon which any and all successes or failures are built. Nothing can be taught until the student's mind is open to learning something new. A biblical parable says seeds sown amid stones and thorns produce little but yield a bounty in good ground. The farmer has to plow before he plants. Likewise, the student must cultivate a desire to learn.

I tell young people that they have to manage that little internal voice that says, "This is garbage. What do I need this for? This is ridiculous. This is stupid. I don't need it." At seminars, I sometimes see scowling kids sitting with their beaming parents. The parents want something for them that they don't want for themselves. Their little voice whispers, "What a waste of a Saturday morning."

I suggest that when that little voice says, "This is BS," tell yourself that BS stands for "blue skies and happy days." At the outset of the learning process, you have to overcome yourself. Don't give in to the tendency to dismiss the importance of a subject. That's why I emphasize that teachers must begin with the end in mind and build the magic of why, because then students will naturally seek the power of how.

Terminology

The teaching process relies on communication. The Latin root of the word communication is communis, which means "to make common." It has been said that great teachers are those who can be understood by someone with whom they have nothing in common. For a coach and player, teacher and student, or parent and child to have quality interaction, they have to be able to speak the same language, which means they have to know the terminology being used and what it means.

Training

Training involves the process of acquiring knowledge and skills. Education requires us to find a person to take us where we are unable to take ourselves, "a coach" to train us. The first two Ts are the first two steps in that training: developing the right attitude and an open mind, and understanding the terminology so that everyone is speaking the same language. And then we progress to the proper use of tools.

Tools

We often hear the expression "the tools of the trade" for any craftsman. There are educational tools as well, and they continue to be useful for a lifetime. One must know how to use them. Anyone can buy a tool, but it's completely different to own it. You own it when you know how to use it consistently and well. That makes you a craftsman. Students do better when they have more tools in the toolbox.

Technique

Technique, simply put, is how you use your tools. A collection of tools isn't enough. The student must learn how best to apply each tool to the task at hand. Technique is the skillful execution of the fundamentals. Technique is critical for success in the information age, as technology seems to outdate itself daily. We must develop our techniques for effectively recording, noting, filing, retrieving information, and planning our work strategically.

BAXTERISM

Take the time it takes, so it takes less time.

Time

There is no shortcut to greatness. We must take the time to do things right, practicing and repeating until we master what we need to learn. My friend Pat Parelli says, "Take the time it takes, so it takes less time." As a coach I simply say, "Do it right or do it again." I tell athletes, "Just trust the process. We're going to get there." We have to take it a step at a time, building the base before advancing. It won't happen overnight. Malcolm Gladwell, in his book Outliers, talks about successful people and the 10,000 hours of work that went into attaining their level of expertise. It takes time! It's like this "good, better, best never let it rest; until you get your good better and your better best."

BAXTERISM

Do it right or do it again.

Just trust the process.

Good, better, best never let it rest; until you get your good better and your better best.

Teamwork

"Life is a team sport." Life is all about the network, about who you know. If you show me your friends, I'll show you your future. Our differences do matter, however. A team needs people with individual talents and dynamic ways of problem solving. And we all need coaches to lead the way.

Creativity can flourish on a team. I think of Walt Disney's Imagineers, and the Vance system of creative thinking. Without creative contributions from team members, the committee mentality can set in. Committees don't do much and what they do, they do very slowly. "If Moses had a committee, the Jews would still be in Egypt." Effective teams do much more than bat around an idea.

Rather, a team needs problem solvers who support one another and people who can function independently and get things done. Teams like that are efficient and effective.

These are the seven building blocks of the success progression. That is the process that young people need—that we all need—in order to execute. Everyone needs to go through that progression. Failure to do so is why talent doesn't translate into performance. Often, I have found, young people don't know what, when, where, why, or how to execute, or else they would. "You don't win silver; you lose gold," I tell them, yet I am convinced that it's not lack of ambition that holds them back. It's lack of basic training.

BAXTERISM

You don't win silver; you lose gold.

These problems involving our schools, our young people, and education in general seem as intertwined as a political plate of spaghetti. You don't know where one starts and another ends. These issues can seem like a knot so tight it seems impossible to pull the strands apart. Academic Gameplan is pulling that knot apart. We're going back to the basics, and restoring the fundamental skills that need to be put in place. If you have a student in your life who could use some help "untying the knot," check out www.agp101.com.*

We need to get back to the elementals of problem solving. When you become a thinker, a communicator, and a competitor, you can do anything you want in your life. When successful people look back at the value of their education, seldom do they first cite all those facts that they mastered in the classroom. Rather, what they draw from every day is something deeper that they learned: the ability to

---

* *See page 175 for a special offer.*

develop a strategic plan based on fundamentals and to execute that plan, conquering self-doubt and adversity

Those fundamentals don't come naturally. They have to be taught. They have to be instilled in young people so that they have something to build upon. "If you do what's natural, you're usually wrong." People sometimes work for 20 years before others call them an "overnight" success. I know the feeling! Success doesn't just happen naturally; in fact, it can be grueling, and one must persevere. Think of a football player in the fourth quarter who is physically, mentally, and emotionally drained. Yet there's still time on that game clock, and his team still needs him.

People who are successful are mentally tough. And being mentally tough requires that you follow through on worthwhile decisions after the emotion of making that decision has passed. Many people start, but very few finish, and the way they finish becomes the definition of their success.

When the game gets tight, when the pressure is on, your skills and endurance will be seriously challenged. Your body says, "It's done, it's over, I can't go anymore." Yet the team is counting on you, and the clock is ticking. For some, the challenge is a speed bump; for others, it's an impasse. But we can get through when we are physically and mentally tough, and when we work with and support one another. While there's still time on the clock, we've got to go for it.

— CLINT'S FIELD NOTE —

Have you ever come back from a day or two of vacation, or sick leave, and whether it was work or school, you felt overwhelmed by responsibilities you needed to attend to? The world seemed to have moved several times as fast while you were away, and now your head is spinning.

Welcome to the life of a student athlete at the highest level. Travel, lifting, practice, meetings, rehab of injury, events with the public, they're all stacked on top of your responsibility to compete in the classroom. This isn't a complaint. It's a reality.

Keeping it all in order can be a challenge. It's all doable, as thousands of athletes demonstrate every year, but without the know-how, it is a real struggle.

BAXTERISM

Control the events in your life, or the events in your life will control you.

Whenever I start to feel overloaded, a "Baxterism" pops into my head: "You guys have got to learn: either you control the events in your life, or the events in your life will control you."

That's why he emphasizes the need to build on the fundamentals. He often says, "It is okay to not understand something, but it's not okay to not understand and not ask a question." It's okay to not know, but it's not okay to accept ignorance. As a coach and as a teacher, he believes in instructing until his students get it, not until he runs out of time. Everything builds on what came before. That's called an installation progression to a football coach.

For students, that means if something's blowing by you, you need to raise your hand and slow down the process. A lot of kids hesitate to ask a question because they don't want to look stupid and have their peers roll their eyes. To raise your hand takes a sense of security and confidence, and at first it's uncomfortable.

But then Coach Baxter follows that up by telling us that "if you do what comes naturally, you're usually wrong." It's natural to sit there and be embarrassed to raise your hand. It's also natural to gravitate toward the back of the classroom where your friends are sitting. It's natural to then never raise your hand at the back of the class, because you don't want to ask an obvious question with all your peers turned around and staring at you. Do what's natural, and you begin at a disadvantage.

BAXTERISM

If you do what comes naturally, you're usually wrong.

If the teachers and administrators work for us as students, it's up to the student to take control and demand clarity. Sitting up front and staying alert helps this process. Remember, the teacher doesn't know what the student doesn't understand. I found that when I sat up front and admitted I didn't see the connection, teachers would come to me afterward and thank me for helping them to communicate better. By speaking up, I also encouraged others in the class to raise their hands.

That's what makes teachers enjoy their job. Otherwise, teachers feel as if they are talking to a wall. They present a lesson and all they see looking back at them from the classroom are blank faces. So they do what's natural and move on to the next concept. Meanwhile, students begin feeling more and more lost. And as one fundamental builds on the previous one, students who don't take control are overcome by the fear that they'll never catch up.

Coach Baxter talks about the panic button that workers can hit on a manufacturing assembly line. If things are going too fast and they get behind, they can hit that button to slow the process and regain control. That's what students do when they raise their hands and ask questions: They slow the teacher down. They take control of their own education.

That's why he emphasizes that daily task list, and note taking, and other basics that allow for strategic planning. And it goes beyond the classroom: It's about being on top of all things in your life, the admirable quality of the most successful and happy people among us. It's all in keeping with the philosophy that if you don't control the events of your life, the events of your life will control you. We observed that in the classroom, and on the field. It's like the major league player swinging at a tee ball: You can always keep working on your swing.

I remember the feeling I had when I realized the power of the planner. When you've got it together that way, people see you as responsible, invested, consistent, and dependable. Others respect you more and see you as a successful leader though you are just using your planner. It's there that you truly do have it all together. I wasn't a terrible student, and I benefited greatly from Academic Gameplan nonetheless. That's a point that Coach Baxter makes repeatedly: No matter how much you know or think you know, you always do better when you master the basics and take control of your life.

CHAPTER 9

Life Skills:

THE EPIPHANY

When I was a high-school sophomore, I put my hand up one day in English class. "Everyone says writing is so important, but can you tell me why?" I asked. The room erupted in laughter.

Maybe my classmates had been wondering the same thing and felt uncomfortable. Or maybe they figured I was hardly in a position to ask. After all, that was the year I was failing every subject. I don't know why they laughed, and neither did the teacher.

"It seems all of you guys think that's funny," the teacher said, "but that is the first intelligent question I've had out of this class." My question couldn't have been more basic. In fact, to some, it might have seemed arrogant, and yet the teacher wholly supported my asking. I wasn't challenging whether I should bother with writing. I simply wanted to know.

How that teacher replied to me—and to the class—has stayed with me for the rest of my life. Imagine if that teacher had laughed at me along with the students. Instead, the teacher reassured me and set me on the path to continue asking questions for the rest of my life. It was a true educator's gift to me, a skill for a lifetime.

Why is writing important? I have taken that teacher's reply and made that discussion part of the Academic Gameplan. In essence: writing matters because it crystallizes your thinking, because it is the only outward way to look at inward thoughts, and because it is a permanent record of humanity's intellect and creativity.

A TRANSFORMING DEFINITION

I've had various epiphanies throughout my coaching career regarding coaching, athletes, and academics. The epiphany of 2007 was one that really changed the magnitude of Academic Gameplan. Even though I've been teaching some of these techniques and fundamentals for 20 plus years, the functional definition for teaching life skills has transformed the program and reshaped its purpose.

Several years ago I was invited to be a copresenter at the NCAA Champs Life Skills Conference. On every NCAA member institution's campus someone is in charge of running the Champs Life Skills program. They gather annually for a conference, with speakers, and I was one of the presenters.

In my presentation, I asked this question: "How would you define life skills?" It seemed nobody could or would give me a functional definition. Many of these people have the words "life skills" on their business cards, with campus titles such as life skills coordinator, or life skills outreach person, but when asked that question, they would usually just come up with an example: shaking hands, introducing yourself, learning how to act in an interview. What I wanted to find out, though, was how one would define a life skill.

I came home from the conference under-impressed and yet passionate about this question of what life skills are. I went to the Champs Life Skills coordinator at Fresno State University.

"You do life skills every day, right?" I asked.

"Yes. I'm the coordinator."

"Okay, then," I said. "What are life skills?" He took a deep breath as if he were about to proclaim the definition, but nothing audible came out.

"Man, I'll have to think about that," he finally said.

"How about this," I said. "If you share your definition of life skills with me, I'll share mine with you." I challenged him to write one, for which he produced a page-and-a-half document. It was eloquent and well-written but, essentially, it said nothing that I could understand.

Any adult you talk to is going to tell you that it's important to teach life skills to kids. Yet if you ask them to define life skills, they cannot. In fact, one person at the conference rolled his eyes and said, "Oh, come on, Coach. It's as easy as what it sounds like, it's skills for life." To which I replied, "Unfortunately, I was well-educated by the Jesuits. One of the things they taught is you cannot define a word with the word itself."

So I spent well over a year creating a functional definition of life skills. I ran it by different people until I got it down to 22 meaningful words. This is what has transformed Academic Gameplan forever. This definition has become the umbrella over everything we teach. If you are preaching the importance of developing life skills in young people, you need to be able to answer these questions: 1) What are life skills? 2) What are the specific life skills you are teaching? And 3), What is your method of delivery? In other words, how are you demonstrating that the term *life skills* is more to you than a political slogan that sounds good to have in an athletic department? In a lot of cases, there's not much substance behind most mission statements.

Here's my *life skills* definition: "**Any technique, tool, or idea that develops into a usable necessity, by connecting to or demonstrating its long-term purpose or usefulness.**" Let's look at each word.

"Life Skills"

Any: there are innumerable potential life skills that can be taught.

Technique, tool, or idea: the skill can be any one or all of these;

That develops: the skill grows over time and evolves;

Into: the skill morphs and changes as it becomes more valuable;

A usable necessity: once you realize its value, you cannot imagine life without it;

By connecting to or demonstrating: there is a teaching process, and the teacher's job lies in building the connection between why and how, and demonstrating that why and how is necessary;

Its long-term purpose and usefulness: life skills last a lifetime.

Until I came up with that definition, I taught techniques that made students more effective, more competitive, which, in turn, brought a broader perspective into laser focus. That allowed me to build the big-enough why. In other words, as I introduce students to a technique, or to a rule, or to a

BAXTERISM

Life Skills: Any technique, tool, or idea that develops into a usable necessity, by connecting to or demonstrating its long-term purpose or usefulness.

fundamental, not only do I show them that it will produce better grades immediately, but I show how this same skill will be useful in various forms for the rest of their lives.

KEEPING YOUR OWN SCORE

I ask my students who keeps score of their grades in math, or history, or any other subject. "The teacher," they invariably answer.

"Why don't you?" I ask.

"Because it's the teacher's job," someone will respond.

"If you want to run a business someday," I ask that person, "who will you want to count the money?"

"I'll do that myself. I don't want to get ripped off."

"So you're telling me," I say, "that you want to handle your money and your finances, but it's not important to keep track of your scores in class?"

That's how I introduce students to the Scoreboard, which is a key piece of our Academic Gameplan "GPS Planning" system. The Student GPS is the name we have given our student planner. We chose GPS because of it's meaning in terms of navigation. In terms of a student navigating an academic career GPS means Guidance, Performance and Strategy. The life skill of keeping your own score in class is the first step in doing personal accounting and keeping detailed records. The students take all the things that are going to be scored throughout the semester, and they lay them out in a scorecard. Then, as they get the results, they fill those in. I

> **BAXTERISM**
>
> Every time a number changes, so does your situation.

emphasize regularly that, "Every time a number changes, so does your situation."

I was a physical education major in college, and I took a class on "Physical Education for Elementary School Students" in which I learned about "basic skills and lead-up games." With students who are at a developmental level, you build basic skills through little lead-up games. As they get good at those, eventually they get good at the big game in the way that T-ball builds skills for baseball.

Using the scorecard, students know where they stand at all times, and they strategize based on number projections. I tell them this is a basic skill and lead-up game for handling all the numbers in their lives, such as the cash flow of a business, or their retirement accounts and their investment portfolio.

That's the purpose of the Scorecard. I tell them, "For the rest of your lives, you are going to make decisions and projections based on numbers." The Scorecard is a lead-up activity that will not only help them organize their academics but all the other numbers in their lives, and it's a developmental activity for consistently keeping records. After all, the scoreboard creates the drama. When I ask my players, "How are you doing in _____?" It's never okay to say, "Fine," "Cool," "Tight," "Strait," or "Pretty good." I want exact numbers in detail. And God forbid they say, "I don't know." They must know exactly where they stand at all times.

THE POWER OF PURPOSE

In teaching such concepts, I demonstrate that they aren't just a way to become more competitive in a subject that may be marginally interesting to the young person. I'm also teaching that these are life skills that will serve them well for many decades.

Students take a math sequence in school, from arithmetic to possibly calculus. In college they can study economics, or national policy. They learn about the gross domestic product, but no one along the way ever taught them personal budgeting or finance. So much of the subject matter that we put forward as an "education" is short-sighted in its approach. Schools don't make the attempt to connect people to the long-term purpose and usefulness of the philosophies, the ideas, and the practices they're putting forward. It's just, "Here's the material. Pass the test. Move on." To truly educate, we must build a bridge to where the information is applicable. If a young person goes to medical school, let's say, or to a trade school, he or she will see how those concepts apply to that field.

By defining life skills, I was able to focus on what I believe is most important, which is building the big-enough why. I can show students, "This is **what** you're going to do. This is **why** you're going to do it. This is **how** you'll use it the rest of your life." Schools are turning out people who have heads that are filled with subjects—and it's just subjects. They lack the savvy to actually manage their lives. The good students schools are turning out are young people who can pass tests, but are they truly equipped for life?

Cavemen taught their children how to build a fire, how to gather wood, how to hunt, how to fish. Essentially, the life skills they taught were survival skills. People have lived in groups since the beginning of the human race and from the group comes education, from the group comes protection, from the group comes safety and security, from the group comes the ability to meet basic human needs.

If you look at Abraham Maslow's Hierarchy of Needs, you will see, at the base of the pyramid are the basic physiological needs: food, clothing, shelter, safety, security. The pinnacle of the Hierarchy of Needs is self-esteem and self-actualization. Here's what I know as an educator of 30 years: There's no shortcut to self-esteem. You cannot do it for the kids. The kids have to go through the process and must experience that success for themselves. As the coach, I cannot play the game for them.

BAXTERISM

There's no shortcut to self-esteem.

In our schools, young people go through algebra, geometry, calculus, and trigonometry, but they do not learn to write a check. They can't tell you about the rule of 72 relating to compounding interest in investments. They can't answer basic questions about personal finance. The educational system sends them out and declares them qualified to earn a paycheck which they are unable to read and handle the day they get it. Without the ability to interpret the line items on that paycheck, how would they ever know how to invest it or even budget it. It's criminal to leave our young people so ill-prepared for adult life.

THE SPIRIT OF COMPETITION

In a program that I've developed, titled "Academic Gameplan 202," one of the lessons is called "Look Both Ways Before You Cross the Street." Many parents have said that, and many children have heard it. Why? It's a basic warning that things in the street move fast, so be wary of the danger inherent in crossing the street. Remember, if you're dead, life skills don't matter.

Yet, high-school graduates and college graduates go into the workforce and we don't tell them to look both ways before they cross the street. They start earning paychecks and blow their money. Many financial planners focus on helping people as they approach retirement so they have enough money to last the rest of their lives. My question is, "Why didn't we teach them these things when they were 16?"

If you don't build the right foundation, the building doesn't stand. Accordingly, if you don't have the right fundamentals, performance suffers. Our schools clearly are failing to build that foundation. They teach subjects but not skills, and they design curriculums lacking variability to meet society's needs currently. Where's the wizard behind the curtain? Who's responsible for leaving this stuff out, and why aren't they changing direction?

When I speak to high-school principals or teachers or coaches, they all agree: They need to teach the rules, fundamentals, and techniques of Academic Gameplan, but they immediately go on to say that they don't have a curriculum slot for it. We seem to lack a curriculum slot for anything that people really need.

We must invest in young people and teach life skills even when they lack the experience to appreciate it. I say two things ad nauseam throughout the teaching process:

BAXTERISM

I don't care about your subjects. I don't care about your grades. I only care about your competitive spirit and your process.

1. "I don't care about your subjects. I don't care about your grades. I only care about your competitive spirit and your process".

2. "I'm not talking to you right now; I'm taking to you 10 years from now!"

To pull a quote from the 1992 movie A Few Good Men:

Col. Nathan Jessup: "You want answers."

Lt. Kaffee: I want the truth.
Col. Nathan Jessup: You can't handle the truth.

But one day they will appreciate the truth and the fact that they were told, which is why I developed the philosophy that a teacher has to become comfortable with the idea that they are a sower and not a reaper. You plant seeds that will grow on another day. When? Why? How? That's not for you to decide. Just keep planting.

> ## BAXTERISM
>
> A teacher has to become comfortable with the idea that they are a sower and not a reaper.

This quote by Gen. Douglas MacArthur is inscribed on the gymnasium at West Point: "On the fields of friendly strife are sown the seeds that on other days and other fields will bear the fruits of victory." That's what education is all about. It's foundation. I now repeat what my father-in-law, Coach Ron McBride, said to Pat Hill before his last game as a senior, "Today's cheers are tomorrow's echoes." Coach Pat Hill was the head coach I worked under at Fresno State: These games are important today, and certainly we want to win, but at the end of the day these results, and these scores, and this pain, or this glory will fade away. What remains will be the spirit of competition and the habit of preparation necessary to win the games that really matter.

WHAT ARE WE MISSING?

We must take a good look at the quality of education in our school systems and at our children's experiences there. We're missing something important. Every cook tastes the soup or the stew while they're making it to see if it needs a little more of this or a little more of that. It's time to inspect the recipe.

College students have long had "general education" as part of their studies. That's where they learn a broad-base curriculum from various disciplines. This forms the basis of a liberal arts education. The fundamentals that must be taught are broader still, and must come earlier, so that we can develop skills for life. We cannot sidestep those fundamentals any longer. It's where we're swinging and missing in school.

Personal finance is one example. We need to teach kids about the risks of credit cards and compounding interest debt, for example, as part of a financial survival course. When Social Security was adopted in 1932, people lived to be 66 at most. Actuaries now calculate that people live until their mid-80s and '90s. Sometimes Social Security has to last a couple for 30 or 40 years and it was not created to do that. Young people must learn to save and invest to create the income streams necessary for lifetime financial security, because Social Security can't be depended on to do it.

If we don't adapt, if we don't adjust to the changes in our society, and if education doesn't emphasize the importance of doing that, we're doomed. Academic Gameplan is my contribution to doing something about an unacceptable situation. We must not accept education as it is. Education must reflect the knowledge, skills, and abilities that a person needs to function in today's society—not post-World War II society or the post-Cold War society, but today. We must stand up for what our children need and make sure they get it. We need to equip our young people for real life, and that is what we offer at www.academicgameplan.com.

I said early in the book that "the number-one job of a teacher is to inspire future learning." In these last 100 years, with the way science, and technology, and information sharing has exponentially advanced, we need to constantly look for ways to adapt. One of the things we tell student athletes in our charge is, "You're going to be an athlete for a part of your life, but you're going to be student for the rest of your life. If you do not embrace this concept we call "being a student," you are dead." A student in our view means the commitment to being a lifelong learner.

For years, kids have heard, "Do your homework. Sit in the front. Turn in your stuff on time. Be diligent." The only problem is that people have difficulty buying into orders, but they are ecstatic about buying into ideas. When they come to understand why something is important, success means a lot more to them than being told by a coach, a teacher, or a parent to "do it because I said so." When a kid asks, "Why?" it's an opportunity to build out the purpose. Be sparing with how often you deliver orders. There are times when you must, but that style can backfire as the mind matures. You're producing people who tend to just respond instead of think.

Twelve-year-olds today are a lot older than 12-year-olds were in 1970. You have to do a better job today than ever before of building a big enough why. If you don't, they're not going to follow you, and you may lose your opportunity to teach them the skills they need for life, leaving them to learn the hard way.

— CLINT'S FIELD NOTE —

My parents are entrepreneurs. They're high-school graduate entrepreneurs, both of them. They started having kids, I think, at 19, probably pretty common for their generation, and immediately got into work and started their own business in the construction industry. They had definite tough times, even though they insulated us from it when we were kids, but I've since learned that they struggled financially at times as they figured out how to make it happen.

My mom used to passionately demand educational performance, with the intent to ultimately excel at college. The one statement that I always remember going back to is, "Look, we had to learn so many lessons the hard way, and I'll be damned if I let you go through the same struggles." She flat out refused to let me go through the challenges that she had to go through to figure stuff out. Same for my dad. That was their motivation.

But when a lot of people my age came out of school, they found that their paycheck was half what they had expected and they couldn't figure out why. They lacked basic skills. How many young people do you think are going to be able to negotiate a car purchase, person to person, when they are used to communicating via text messages? As for me, I was extremely technically savvy. I could tear apart a corporate financial statement but knew nothing about how to manage my credit score. Was I really avoiding the school of hard knocks that way?

I started my real estate and finance career in November 2008, the depth of the recession. Everyone was neck-deep in the mess, and no one knew what was going on. This is when attorneys were going to real estate agents to ask what a short sale was and how it worked. Now, the opposite is true. Most of the transactions I've done have involved some sort of distress and financial hardship, whether the transaction involved a multimillionaire or someone making $30,000 a year.

To get business, my sister, Shayla, and I started going door to door to get refinance deals. You would be shocked at the questions, or lack thereof, that people were asking when it came to refinancing. They didn't even know where to start. Everyone was acting out of fear and emotion instead of objective analysis to find the best scenario. We would offer people refinances, and then I would offer some objective analysis of the pros and cons of the scenario offered under the government relief program. They didn't want to hear it. They just wanted to be told it was okay. They didn't want to have to think, or learn, or understand the decision they were going to make. Where were their problem-solving skills? "Ignorance isn't the fact that you don't know the answer. It's the fact that you don't realize there's a question" is what Coach Baxter used to tell me.

BAXTERISM

Ignorance isn't the fact that you don't know the answer. It's the fact that you don't realize there's a question.

Whether highly educated, or not, I regularly see people encountering struggles and hard knocks because they lack basic financial understanding, basic negotiation, basic budgeting, and basic problem-solving skills that can be easily taught and learned before there is a problem. Coach Baxter taught us to question everything while keeping an open mind for the answer. He drilled into our heads the idea that "it's OK to not understand; but it's not OK to not understand and not ask a question." President Kennedy said, "An error doesn't become a mistake until you refuse to correct it." Unfortunately, solving these issues in education seems easier to put off, rather than to deal with now. How long will we wait until these errors become major mistakes in our society? It's simple and basic. I am thankful for my parents and their influence on me and I am thankful for college football because I got to train for 1800 days under a man like Coach Baxter. Even though I left college with two degrees, I can tell you that the majority of my practical education came from my parents and my coaches. I am a thinker, a communicator, and a competitor thanks to them.

When it came to us consistently taking care of our business, Coach Baxter used to say, "Look. Today is the tomorrow you talked about yesterday. What are you waiting for? Divine intervention?!" In other words, just take care of business and get it done. In fact a Baxterism that remains a tremendous nugget in my daily life is his key to organization. He says, "the key to organization is to handle every little thing immediately." He means little things because little things left unattended become major all consuming time robbers and obstacles in productivity.

BAXTERISM

Today is the tomorrow you talked about yesterday.

The key to organization is to handle every little thing immediately.

It is crazy to me that people won't pay a penny for a solution, but they'll liquidate their life savings to purchase the cure. Practicing the fundamentals is the solution, and the outstanding academic achievement of Coach Baxter's athletes proves it.

CHAPTER 10

Conclusion:

"I'M MAD AS HELL..."

In the 1976 movie *Network*, a once-popular news anchor, jaded by all the trash that his network was peddling as worthy of attention, makes a desperate public appeal in what was to be his final broadcast: "I'm mad as hell and I'm not going take this anymore!" It's a call to action. Soon viewers nationwide are shouting his words out of windows; such is the public's pent-up frustration.

Academic Gameplan started as a set of rules, fundamentals, and techniques, and for years it served my student athletes well. It was a humble attempt to put them in a position to be more competitive in all areas of life, and mostly on the academic side. Since then it has grown to focus on the mastery of life skills as students discover purpose.

Clint and I both were told by our parents that higher education was non-negotiable. Both of us were raised by parents who were not college graduates but who believed strongly that it was not an option to skip college. They were sure it would be our ticket to success. Each of us now holds a master's degree—and we know that when you enter the work force, "you better have substance behind your smile," and that substance generally comes through competition and competitive greatness in all areas of our lives.

BAXTERISM

You better have substance behind your smile.

There are only two ways to learn: shock or repetition.

In my thirty years of coaching, I have found that "there are only two ways to learn: shock or repetition." You can tell kids the stove is hot a hundred times, or they can touch it once.

A lot of hot stoves await the touch of young adults graduating from college. They can get burned financially, for example, and in so many other ways. But who in school has taught them how to do strategic planning? Nobody. Who taught them how to make a prioritized daily task list? Nobody. Who taught them how to take notes? Nobody. Who taught them how to keep records and files? Nobody. Who taught them how to keep score and make projections based on numbers and trends? Nobody. Who asked them to answer this fundamental question: "Who are you, and what do you represent?" Who taught them the basics of personal finance and how to strategically deal with their paycheck? Nobody.

Nobody!

"Schools are teaching subjects, not skills". The *Harvard Business Review* reported that the number-one criterion in hiring an employee is the ability to communicate. Technology is breeding young people right now who learn to communicate via text messaging. Who is teaching the simple art of face to face conversation, challenge, or confrontation? Who is teaching them how to negotiate the purchase of a house or car? You don't learn to negotiate or handle confrontation when you're sending texts from a distance, or you're out to dinner with three friends, and each of you is looking at your phone, and you're not looking someone in the eye.

> **BAXTERISM**
>
> Schools are teaching subjects, not skills.

Our educational system is letting people cross the street without looking both ways. It is overpromising and under delivering. I want to extend a challenge to all principals and superintendents. When you're evaluating your teachers, bring them in one at a time, and just ask them one simple question: *"Why should your subject stay in the curriculum long-term, and why should you be the one teaching it?"* If they can't answer the question, don't hire them.

HITTING THE BULL'S-EYE

In every recruiting presentation, when we're sitting in the prospect's home, we explain the Academic Gameplan logo. I drew the logo myself in 1994 while I was working at Tulane University. I was teaching Academic Gameplan to our football players, never thinking that it was going to become a corporate logo for a company helping students all over the country.

First and foremost, I felt that successful people have to have a target. Then I came up with this idea of separating students into red, yellow, and green, the colors of a traffic light.

The outer circle is red and unfortunately it is the largest. Red represents "stop." It is the color for the large group of people who are going nowhere and haven't accomplished much. Of the seven billion people on earth today, over one billion of them cannot read or write their native language. Bill Gates talks about "the bottom two billion," the third of the world's population that struggles to get by on less than two dollars a day. For those souls, education is not an opportunity.

But many who do have the opportunity are missing out. The red circle in the logo represents those people who don't come to school or, if they do, don't have their homework or come late or sit in the back of the class. They talk, they act out, they don't take notes, they're unprepared. They comprise the red group. Unfortunately, that's the largest group of people.

The next largest group is represented by the yellow circle. In discussing this with students, I ask, "Okay, what do you do at a yellow light?" Someone says, "I slow down." Someone else says he speeds up at a yellow light to get through. "Okay," I say, "you guys might as well just exchange your insurance information now, because you're going to meet at the intersection someday." The yellow light is where the accidents happen because it means different things to different people. The yellow students are inconsistent. They're getting through education and having some success, but for every success they take a step backward too.

Then come the greens. The greens are the people who are going places and doing things. They are goal oriented. Green means "go," and it's also the color of money and the color of growth. Unfortunately, that is the smallest group of people.

If you put the greens anywhere, they'll be successful. You can put them in any school. You can put them with any teacher. They're going to work hard enough and ask enough critical questions to ultimately become successful. The greens succeed in spite of you. They succeed in spite of the coach. They succeed in spite of the teacher. They can actually overcome bad instruction. They're highly motivated people who don't take no for an answer and they persevere against adversity.

The reds and the yellows succeed because of you. The critical question to always ask is: "How are we serving the reds and the yellows?" In other words, are we seeing the value in them? Are we digging to find the pearl in the oyster? The reds and the yellows need effective instruction, or they will be lost.

Imagine an announcement over the school speakers in which the principal says, "Will all the students who had below a 2.0, or at least two Fs on their transcript, please report to the gym after school for a group picture? And any teachers who would like to be in this photo, please report as well." Who do you suppose would show up? Any students? Any teachers? *Nobody wants to be in that picture.*

Imagine a different announcement: "After school, all honor roll students please report to the gym for a group picture, along with any teachers who would like to be in that picture with them." You can bet that the gym will be bustling after school that day.

For me, I want to be in the picture with the reds and the yellows. Those are the people I know I can help. It's with those students that we can make the biggest difference. Our schools are failing them, and we must stand up and shout that "we're mad as hell, and we're not going to take this anymore." I, for one, want to be there for them, and with them. Keep in mind that when you say every day with these young people is a challenge, that's a bigger understatement than Noah saying, "Looks like rain." It's not easy but the rewards for breakthroughs are incredible.

In the logo, the green is the bull's-eye because those people are on the inner circle. They're inside looking out and they're successful. They're goal oriented. They have demonstrated mastery of details. And that is why, in the logo, the bull's-eye dots the *i* in Academic Gameplan. Details matter! It's a plan to give students a fighting chance to win in the *game of academics*.

"AND THEN..."

In my professional career, and with Academic Gameplan, I strive to be the teacher that I wish I'd had. I want to be the teacher that I wish I'd had in algebra, who would have inspired me with the beauty and logic of numbers and made it clear to me why I needed that skill for the rest of my life. I want to be the teacher that I wish I'd had in history, who would have connected and demonstrated for me how the events of long ago remained forever relevant, a teacher who doesn't insist on memorizing dates and names but, rather, on the significance of the events and how they continue to affect us today.

I want to be the teacher I wish I'd had in science, and literature, and all the many disciplines of humanity. I've spent my career to become the teacher who explains the why and the how and who motivates students to be learners for a lifetime, striving to make the best of themselves.

I was watching the Biography Channel on TV one rainy Saturday morning with my wife, Jill. We watched two or three episodes in a row.

"Every one of these stories is the same," I told her. "We hear about these people's lives, and in every story you hear the words 'and then...' That's me," I observed. That was the epiphany of 1998 that got me started on writing and formalizing Academic Gameplan. "That's what I'm here to do. That's why I coach. These kids come thinking they're going to play college football and get a degree. Then we sit in the classroom and start teaching rules, fundamentals, and techniques of how to win at the game of school."

And then...

My desire as a teacher and a coach is to really be the "and then ..." story. One day when the young people whom I have served look back at their turning point, I want them to be able to say, "I was just going along, not sure what I was doing, and then a coach came to sit at my dining room table. And then he told me what I would need to do to succeed in life."

"And then..."

— CLINT'S FIELD NOTE —

Of all of the "Baxterisms" that I recall, one stands out for me. He invariably would say it on Friday nights at the special teams meeting before the game. It's the most intense meeting of the week. When I say "intense," no words can describe how demanding he is when it comes to preparation. He does not compromise and he does not moderate. You'd better know what you're doing and what you're talking about or you don't play. Coach Baxter demands everyone's attention and he puts guys on the spot. They have to stand up, in front of the whole team and coaching staff, and describe their role, their assignment, the challenges that the opponent presents, and how they're going to complete their job to help the team win. You are also expected to know any role that you back up. When speaking, he rants, "Volume reflects confidence," and your voice better not crack or quiver as you respond at the top of your lungs. There's this aura of intensity in the room because tomorrow is game day, and no one wants to let the team down.

BAXTERISM

You must keep your eyes on the target, your feet gaining ground, and your hands on all blocks.

Every Friday Coach Baxter never failed to say, "You must keep your eyes on the target, your feet gaining ground, and your hands on all blocks." He said it again, and again, and again. And he yelled it. He leaned forward, and his hands came down with every syllable. He pounded that point into us.

As a player, I figured, "Yeah, I get it, Coach. We're just going to look at the guy who's got the ball. We're going to keep running so we get closer to him. If anyone gets in our way, well, we're going to keep our hands on those people to make sure that we have a clear path to the ball. I get it already! Eyes on the target, feet gaining ground, hands on all blocks. That's how we're going to play the game of football ..."

I played my last college football game on December 31, 2007, and it was shortly before the game that I last heard him say those words. Then, in March 2013 (10 years after I met Coach Baxter), I was out jogging, trying to think through a complex business problem. Should we kill the deal, or push through? I was running into the wind, and I felt exhausted. I felt like giving up.

And then..., from somewhere in the wind, I heard that old familiar voice: "Keep your eyes on the target, your feet gaining ground, and your hands on all blocks!"

Thanks, Coach.

BAXTERISM

And Then...

Baxterisms

For your convenience, use and entertainment I have listed the "Baxterisms" in the order that they occurred in the book. In Chapter two, Clint introduced this concept. Until the writing of this book, I was never formally aware that there was such a term. It's hilarious to me that this idea even exists. These "Baxterisms" are phrases and statements that I use regularly to inspire, challenge and summarize my philosophy into a meaningful nugget that a student can remember. Obviously, it has worked. I'm sure that if you have reached this point you have highlighted many of them but can't remember what page they are on. Well, there are "Baxterisms" and "Super-Baxterisms." A "Super-Baxterism" is one that is a real zinger and stands out among the rest as something that is a stand-alone concept with major impact. I hear the players and coaches that I work with saying them over and over again. The supers are bolded in the list below.

1. **"This is college football, not football college."**

2. "The universal principal of coaching is, the neighbor always has to tell your kid to choke up on the bat."

3. **"It's not about the hype, it's about the prep."**

4. "Champions love the work and want-to-be's love the idea."

5. "I am not talking to you right now; I am talking to you ten years from now."

6. "A coach is a person that takes you where you are unable to take yourself."

7. **"That's a violation of the anti-simplicity rule."**

8. "Truly successful people live their life with an attitude of gratitude."

9. **"Life is a team sport."**

10. **"Trying is just losing with honor."**

11. "I don't believe in learning disabilities, I believe in learning differences."

12. "The number-one job of a teacher is to inspire future learning."

13. "The Magic of Why and the Power of How."

14. "Don't do anything because I said so; do it because you know why."

15. "It's OK to not understand; but it's not OK to not understand and not ask a question."

16. **"When you change the way you look at things, the things you look at change." Dr. Wayne Dyer**

17. "People buy into ideas, not orders."

18. "There's no reason for failure when success is offered every day."

19. "Manage your little voice."

20. "You're going to be an athlete for part of your life but you're going to be a student for the rest of your life."

21. **"You show me your friends, and I'll show you your future."**

22. "Talent is the raw material technique is the finished product."

23. "Slow and right is better than fast and wrong."

24. "To solve a problem, you go from chaos to concept. Then process to product."

25. "The Deadline Triggers the Process" (MOST USED OF ALL).

26. "There's more to a person than his transcripts."

27. "People who don't read have no distinct advantage over people who can't read."

28. "Take the time it takes, so it takes less time."

29. "Do it right or do it again."

30. "Just trust the process."

31. "Good, better, best never let it rest; until you get your good better and your better best."

32. "You don't win silver; you lose gold."

33. "Control the events in your life or the events in your life will control you."

34. "If you do what comes naturally, you're usually wrong."

35. "Life Skills: Any technique, tool, or idea that develops into a usable necessity, by connecting to or demonstrating its long-term purpose or usefulness."

36. "Every time a number changes, so does your situation."

37. "There is no shortcut to self-esteem."

38. "I don't care about your subjects or your grades. I only care about your competitive spirit and your process".

39. "A teacher has to become comfortable with the idea that they are a sower and not a reaper."

40. **"Ignorance isn't the fact that you don't know the answer. It's the fact that you don't realize there's a question."**

41. **"Today is the tomorrow you talked about yesterday."**

42. "The key to organization is to handle every little thing immediately."

43. "You better have substance behind your smile."

44. "There are only 2 ways to learn. Shock or repetition."

45. "Schools are teaching subjects, not skills."

46. **"Keep your eyes on the target, your feet gaining ground, and your hands on all blocks."**

47. "The 7 success Ts are Attitude, Terminology, Training, Tools, Technique, Time and Teamwork."

48. **"And then…"**

Coach John Baxter:

Coach Baxter and his wife, Jill, have two daughters, Kelly and McKenzie. His father-in-law, Ron McBride, is the former Head Football Coach at the University of Utah and Weber State University.

Born June 28, 1963, raised in Chicago, Illinois, and a 1981 Graduate of Loyola Academy. He earned his bachelor's degree in Physical Education from Loras College in 1985 and then his master's degree in Higher Education from Iowa State in 1987. A career college football coach, Coach Baxter has established a nationally prominent reputation as both a teacher and coach.

He was named the 2011 National Special Teams Coordinator of the Year while at USC and is known for developing some of the most prolific special teams units in the game of college football. His players have been consistently lauded for their academic and athletic achievements. The players that he has had the opportunity to mentor reads like a directory of super achievers.

Along with his coaching duties Coach Baxter has authored and copyrighted the highly-successful and nationally-acclaimed program, "The Academic Gameplan™." His innovative and comprehensive life-skills program teaches students the rules, fundamentals and techniques to succeed in the classroom. "Academic Gameplan," is used in homes and at schools throughout the country. The program he created was the key ingredient for the phenomenal academic success of the Fresno State football program. Going from the nations worst graduation rate in 1996, Baxter's tenure produced 141 Academic All-WAC players and an NCAA APR score nearly 20 percentage points higher than the national average.

He is a featured speaker and community servant and was selected as the Clovis, California, Citizen of the Year in 2006.

His coaching resume highlights are:

2010: Associate Head Football Coach, Special Teams Coordinator and Tight End Coach, University of Southern California

1997 – 2009: Associate Head Football Coach, Special Teams Coordinator and Tight End Coach, California State University-Fresno

1994 – 1996: Special Teams Coordinator and Tight End Coach, Tulane University

1992 – 1993: Special Teams Coordinator and Running Back Coach, The University of Maryland

1990 – 1991: Special Teams Coordinator and Tight End Coach, University of Arizona

1989: Special Teams Coordinator and Linebacker Coach, University of Maine

1988: Graduate Assistant Coach, University of Arizona

1986 – 1987: Graduate Assistant Coach, Iowa State University

1981 – 1985: Undergraduate Assistant Coach, Loras College

Clint Stitser:

Born and raised in Reno, Nevada. 2003 Graduate of McQueen High School, Bachelor of Science in Finance (2007); awarded the Dean's Medal as the top graduate from the Craig School of Business. MBA in General Management (2008); honored as a top-five Graduate from the Craig School of business. 2010: recognized as a member of the NFL All Rookie Team as a Place Kicker. Accomplished real estate sales, investment, and lending professional. Coordinator of Student Outreach at Academic Gameplan. Husband to Christie Stitser, and father to two daughters, Avery and Brynn.

After being recruited by Coach John Baxter in 2003, Clint attended Fresno State as a Placekicker (2003-2008). While playing for Coach Baxter, Clint was a record-breaking student-athlete on and off the field, setting multiple records academically and athletically while receiving national recognition for his work.

Subsequent to his retirement from the NFL, Clint has dedicated his time and effort to making significant impact on students everywhere through Coach Baxter's Academic Gameplan. It's his desire to help every student reap the benefits of competitive greatness that he gleaned from the coaches who impacted his life.

How can you use this book?

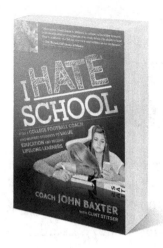

MOTIVATE

EDUCATE

THANK

INSPIRE

PROMOTE

CONNECT

I Hate School is available in bulk quantities and at special discounts for corporate, institutional, and educational purposes. To learn more please contact our Special Sales team at:

1.877.808.PLAN • **agpsuccess@academicgameplan.com**
Ihateschoolthebook.com • **Promo Code: "Bulk Pricing"**

How Coach's System Revolutionizes Student Performance

A step by step process that utilizes "guided discovery" to help your student(s) take ownership of the rules, fundamentals, and techniques to the game of school.

Phase 1: Why School?

Phase 2: Attitude Development

Phase 3: The Academic Bat

Phase 4: Winning the Situations

Don't leave your child behind!

They don't come out of the womb knowing this stuff and schools don't teach it. To learn more, and to take advantage of special discounts offered to those who have purchased and read this book, please go to **AGP101.com** and use Promo Code:

"The Book"

Printed in the USA
CPSIA information can be obtained
at www.ICGtesting.com
JSHW011417160824
R13664500003B/R136645PG68134JSX00036B/15